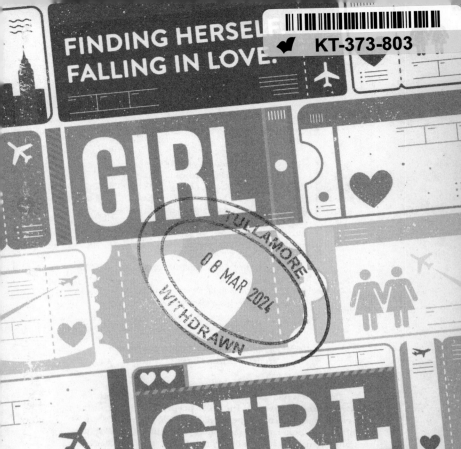

FINDING HERSEL
FALLING IN LOVE.

GIRL

GIRL

LUCY SUTCLIFFE

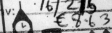

SCHOLASTIC

Scholastic Children's Books
An imprint of Scholastic Ltd
Euston House, 24 Eversholt Street, London, NW1 1DB, UK
Registered office: Westfield Road, Southam, Warwickshire, CV47 0RA
SCHOLASTIC and associated logos are trademarks and/
or registered trademarks of Scholastic Inc.

First published in the UK by Scholastic Ltd, 2016

ISBN 978 1407 15415 2

A CIP catalogue record for this book is available
from the British Library.

Printed by CPI Group (UK) Ltd, Croydon, CR0 4YY
Papers used by Scholastic Children's Books are made from
wood grown in sustainable forests.

3 5 7 9 10 8 6 4

www.scholastic.co.uk

This book is dedicated to my Mum, my
Dad and my brother Laurie – for not only
encouraging me to think sideways, but also
back to front and upside down.

In times of sadness or distress, I have often sought comfort in the idea that the best is yet to come. To me, the "best" doesn't have to be the glitz and the glamour of some star-studded, bright-lights premiere where I'd walk down the red carpet in a custom Vera Wang ballgown and everyone is screaming my name. The "best" can be a steaming hot cup of coffee early one November morning when it's still dark outside and all I can see when I look up is the fluorescent amber glow of street lights against the slow rise of dawn. The best can be when I'm swimming in the sea against the current, the warm waves lapping at my face, my heart pounding, adrenaline coursing through me, just breathing, floating, drifting. The best can be the way snow settles over a busy city; quietly, slowly, then all at once, covering the world in a bright white blanket of the same clean slate.

If you're sat here with this book in your hands and shaking your head sadly, convinced that nobody in the world cares about you, let me tell you this: they do. There are people in the world that will love and support you – no matter who you are. Even if the idea of being loved feels like it couldn't be further away from your grasp. Even if the thought of getting out of bed in the morning sometimes makes you feel sick. Even if your hands shake in public places and your voice wobbles when you speak to people you don't know. No matter your gender or sexuality – you will be loved. You are good enough. There are people in this world that are cheering you on as you round every corner and jump every hurdle, willing you forward, hoping you'll make it. You might not have met them just yet, but they're there, I promise. You are not alone. And if you take only one thing from reading this book, let it be this: it gets better.

Lucy
x

IS THERE SOMETHING WRONG WITH ME?

Once a year, during the summer term, our school headmaster Mr Walker would ceremoniously unlock the gates to the woodland area behind the playing field. There was a small clearing right in the middle, and Year 6 were allowed to eat there at lunchtimes.

Mr Walker was a vast, terrifying man with a booming voice and a huge belly which hung over his belt like an over-cooked muffin. A staunch Christian (it was a Church of England school), he would insist on eating his lunch with the Year 6 students to ensure they wouldn't be 'tempted by sin'. Whenever someone misbehaved in class, Mr

Walker looked them dead in the eyes and described what it was like in Hell for naughty children. I once overheard him telling my classmate Oliver that if he didn't stop talking, flames from the Eternal Fire would burn his mouth clean off. Oliver didn't speak for the rest of the day.

At lunchtimes, the woodland clearing would come alive with chatter and gossip. People would bring cards, or play ball games – one boy even used to bring up his guitar – but as soon as Mr Walker arrived, everyone would fall quiet. The Year 6 students would eat their sandwiches in silence, chewing anxiously, avoiding eye-contact.

I was sitting alone one break time, as I often did, perched by the gate under the huge willow tree, munching on my sandwiches (cheese with tomato ketchup – a winning combination for an eight-year-old). I envied the Year 6 students, with their brightly coloured lunchboxes and customized rucksacks. They seemed so effortlessly cool. I imagined sitting in the clearing with them, chatting and laughing about the music they listened to and the TV shows they'd watched last night. I wondered what it would be like to be popular, with dozens and dozens of friends.

The boys in my year were playing football. They'd set up makeshift goalposts with their sweatshirts at each end of the field, and every now and then, someone would kick the ball and it would hit the pile of sweatshirts, sending them flying. A tirade of insults would follow. It was swelteringly hot, and everyone was irritable.

From my spot under the low-hanging branches, I watched as a rowdy debate between two boys got more and more heated.

"You didn't even try to save that one! I don't even know why you bother playing!"

"Uh, maybe because it's too hot to actually DO anything?"

"Oh, is it too hot for you? You absolute wimp. You're so *gay!*"

The school bell rang and everyone fell silent. Mr Walker emerged from the clearing with

3

a face like thunder, a tiny piece of ham sandwich dangling ominously from his chin. "My office, NOW," he roared. The two boys froze.

I went to line up by the classroom door, absorbed by my thoughts. I'd never heard the word 'gay' before. It must be something truly horrible, judging by the way Mr Walker had reacted.

I turned to my friend Alexa and asked her if she knew.

"What, you don't know what gay means?!" She laughed nervously. She clearly had no clue either.

A playground monitor, who had been sitting on a nearby bench immersed in a gossip magazine, looked up. "You kids don't need to know," she said, with a smirk.

We filed into the classroom. What *did* gay mean? Why did it make people behave so strangely? And why didn't anyone want to tell me? I felt suddenly ashamed, as if just thinking about it was going to get me into trouble.

✈

Later that evening, after school, I was sitting in the back garden playing with my guinea pigs when the doorbell rang.

I went to the door and peered through the peephole on my tiptoes. A boy from my school, Dom, was standing there. I was taken aback. Dom was one of the popular kids – all the girls in my class were crazy about him. So what was he doing here? I looked through the peephole again. He was wearing bright green wellies and had his arms folded. He looked very serious.

I opened the door cautiously. "Hi?"

He said nothing. We stood there awkwardly, staring at each other. After a long, long silence, he suddenly blurted out, "So, do you want to be my girlfriend?"

I laughed, out of shock more than anything. "Erm . . . no thanks."

"Why not? Come on, you know you want to."

"Nah, I don't think so."

My dad popped his head around the kitchen door. "What's going on?"

Neither Dom nor I said anything for a moment.

"You should probably go," I said with a nervous laugh. "I'm cleaning my room, so I'm a bit busy."

"You're not cleaning your room, liar. I'm not leaving until you say yes."

My dad came striding down the hallway. "I'm pretty sure she said no," he said, glaring.

Dom glared back.

Dad shut the door firmly in Dom's face, then turned to me with a sympathetic smile. "Don't ever let someone make you do something you don't want to do."

My mind was reeling. Dom had made me feel so uncomfortable, but I still felt vaguely embarrassed, and almost apologetic, that I had turned him down. Had I hurt his feelings? Would he ever want to talk to me again? I couldn't help feeling guilty.

I spent the next day at school trying to avoid Dom at all costs. I didn't see him all morning and hid in the library at lunchtime, worried that I'd bump into him on the playground. But when English class rolled around that afternoon, he plonked himself down at a table right in front of mine. I shrunk into my chair and pretended to be immersed in the book I was reading.

I felt so uncomfortable. Was he going to say something to me, or would I have to avoid him for ever? I began to question why I wasn't interested in him, when most of the other girls in my class clearly were. Come to think of it, they were *all* boy crazy. So why wasn't I? He wasn't bad looking, and he seemed to have an OK personality. Was there something wrong with me?

Suddenly I felt angry. *That could have been your only chance to fall in love, and you just blew it*, I thought to myself. I stared at the back of Dom's head, trying to figure out what it would be like to kiss him. Maybe it would be like in the movies, with a sunset behind us and a dramatic soundtrack to match. *Still gross*, I thought, shuddering.

As I fell asleep that night, I told myself that love would come again – and that next time, I would be prepared. I had read about love in *Little*

Women – it wasn't supposed to come easily, that was the whole point. Jo rejects Laurie because she prefers Professor Bhaer. All I had to do was wait for my Professor Bhaer.

After all, love is something rare; something not to be rushed.

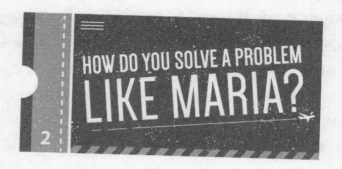

Growing up, I was boundlessly optimistic. Just as I was sure that I would fall in love some day, I was also sure that I would find true friendship, with people that 'got' me. The real me.

The first encounter that I remember with bullies outside of books was when I was five.

My parents' busy work schedules meant they didn't have time to do the school run, so every morning, my mum dropped me off at the childminder's house. Here, to take my mind off how much I missed them, I retreated into my imagination. I devoured book after book, immersing myself in the worlds of Enid Blyton,

Jacqueline Wilson, C.S. Lewis, J.K. Rowling and Roald Dahl (I was an unusually quick reader!), surrounding myself with characters and places that only existed between the pages in my hands. To me, these worlds were as real as the one I lived in – they were just harder to see.

Once I'd finished a book, there wasn't much else for me to do. While my childminder was getting ready upstairs, I'd flick listlessly through the TV channels, or stare out of the window and count the cars that went by. For a while, this was my morning routine – that is, until I discovered something that changed my life.

I called it 'colour catching'.

Perched on the childminder's sofa, I would stare, unblinking, at the naked light bulb on the ceiling. As soon as I looked away, bright coloured blobs would appear in front of my eyes. Red and green splotches would float by lazily, followed by a scattering of bright pinks and yellows. It was my job to catch them using any means I could (a fishing net, a bucket, my hands), chasing them across the room in gymnastic-style jumps from the sofa to the armchair, armchair to the table, table to the floor. I was convinced that I had magical eyes, a special power that no one else could know about.

One morning, having planned out the details of an extremely risky leap from the coffee table to the armchair, the living room door suddenly opened. A boy and a girl walked in, both a few years older than me.

"Lucy, this is James and Bethany, they're brother and sister," said the childminder, Christine, bustling in behind them. She looked up from her handbag and stopped. "What are you doing?"

I stood, frozen on the coffee table, knees bent, one foot up in the air, arms outstretched. Bethany sniggered loudly and raised an eyebrow.

"Weirdo," muttered James.

Over the weeks that followed, I tried my best to befriend James and Bethany, asking them about themselves and chatting away about my favourite topics – Harry Potter, mainly:

"You're supposed to add fluxweed to the cauldron before knotgrass – and it *has* to be picked when there's a full moon..."

"... but I mean, if you think about it, Snape was just trying to *protect* Harry..."

But despite my best efforts, they seemed entirely disinterested. James in particular took a strong dislike to me, calling me names and throwing my things across the room when Christine wasn't looking. I already knew mean people existed, of course – my books had warned me about the White Witches and Voldemorts of the world – but meeting them in real life was a shock. I'd lived in a bubble where everyone was friendly – and James and Bethany had burst it.

It took me a long time to realize that me being myself was both the solution and the problem. James couldn't see into my world of colour-catching, witches, and fire-breathing dragons. He didn't understand it, so he felt threatened – and lashed out.

Primary school wasn't much better. I struggled to fit in amongst the sports fanatics and maths whizzes, choosing instead to sit in the library and read or write stories at lunchtimes. Most of my classes were just about bearable, with the exception of PE – the one lesson I despised. I was embarrassingly bad at anything involving hand-eye coordination, so being picked last for teams became almost routine. Even the teachers would sigh and shrug their shoulders as I failed to catch the umpteenth ball thrown in my direction.

The only lesson I truly enjoyed was English, with Mrs Robinson – my favourite teacher. She was kind but firm, with endless patience and a knack for boosting self-confidence in even the shyest of children. She told me I had a wonderful imagination and a talent for story writing, and she was one of the only teachers who ever made me feel like I might be good at something.

But despite Mrs Robinson's encouragement, I was becoming increasingly lonely. My best friend Rachel went to a different school so I could only see her at weekends, my little brother Laurie was too young for my games, and my pen pal, Ashley, lived an ocean away in New York. My activities were solitary. I started cycling, riding my rickety pink bike around my street in circles, my favourite doll, Katy, propped up in the wicker basket at the front. I'd sing as I pedalled – usually classics from my favourite films. "Hoooow do you soooolve a problem like Mariaaa?" I'd bellow at the top of my lungs. Goodness knows what the neighbours must have thought.

One afternoon, some girls who lived on my street decided it would be funny to run away whenever they saw me. "She's coming!" they screamed as they rushed to hide behind a wall, laughing at me as I whooshed past. I pretended not to hear them, chatting loudly to Katy about the weather and looking pointedly in the other direction.

I thought it was strange that they didn't want to join in. I assumed it was because they had other interests, but in reality they probably just thought I was weird. I suppose I was, in a way – not many kids my age wore wigs made out of string (more on this later!) or talked out loud to their dolls. But 'changing to fit in' had never once occurred to me. Perhaps it was the way I was brought up, or perhaps it was something more inherent – either way, it never crossed my mind. I was Lucy Sutcliffe, and they could take it or leave it.

My parents were my ultimate support system. Whenever I came home from school, feeling hurt by something someone had done or sad about a comment someone had made, my mum would pull me into a hug.

"Always respond with kindness, my love," she would say with a sympathetic smile.

"Why should I? They're horrible."

"Because otherwise, they've won."

I knew she was right.

As time went on, I became more and more engrossed in the make-believe worlds I was reading about in books and seeing on the television. I was quickly making my way through the entire children's section at my local library and was constantly begging the librarian to bring in more books. I lived for Anne Shirley's adventures in Avonlea. I longed to have Pippi Longstocking as a best friend. Pollyanna's everlasting optimism propelled me forwards on my loneliest days. And although I was still young, I knew that the strong female leads I was reading about were the embodiment of what it meant to be your own person. Through them I imagined a better, bigger, braver me: self-assured, loud and inspiring, unashamedly myself. Imaginary Lucy didn't care about mean people – she had more important things to do.

My most prized possession during these years was a video camera that my family had given me for my birthday. My friend Rachel and I spent countless weekends writing and filming our own silly little skits and spoofs. Here I *could* be loud. I *was* brave. We'd craft slapdash costumes out of blankets and clothes pegs, then walk through the village dressed as our characters – scullery maids, TV presenters, and, more than once, Simon Cowell in drag – trying to keep a straight face as we made eye contact with passers-by.

We spent hours working on our scripts, sitting cooped up in my room stuffing Thorntons toffee into our faces, using a thesaurus to pick out the most obscure words we could possibly find.

"I need another word for 'walk.'"

"What's the sentence?"

"They walk to the shops."

"OK, how about ambulate?" Rachel said, thumbing through the thesaurus.

"They AMBULATE to the shops?!"

"Oh no, wait, I've found a good one. Toddle. They can toddle to the shops."

We fell about laughing.

Then came the bit I loved best: editing the films on Rachel's ancient PC. I was used to storytelling the old-fashioned way, with words on a page and a pen in my hand, but telling a story visually, with film clips and sound effects, was even more exciting. My dad, who made animations for a living, showed me how it worked step by step. I loved every second of it, and I decided right then and there that video editing was a job I would love to have some day.

I dreamt endlessly about the future, and turned my fantasies into art through short stories and screenplays, encouraged by the support from my parents, Mrs Robinson, and Rachel. I pictured myself as a top-level film editor, cutting together video clips at the speed of light. I imagined what my edit suite would be like; a state-of-the-art studio tucked away in the Hollywood Hills, with shelf after shelf jam-packed full of Oscars. I thought about my co-workers' faces when they saw what I could do; awe-struck and inspired, impressed by my talents, clapping and whooping as I loaded up more reels of film, ready for round two. I knew it was possible if I put my mind to it. My imagination was telling me to hold on, so that's exactly what I did.

Besides – why listen to the Jameses and Bethanys of the world, when you could listen to the Rachels and Mrs Robinsons?

HERMIONE GRANGER

3

I was five when the first Harry Potter book came out, and Hermione Granger became my hero overnight. She was everything I wanted to be – smart, logical, independent, and true to herself. I used Hermione's quiet determination as my inspiration; I knew I could be just as powerful as her.

I read all the books myself, but insisted that my dad read them aloud to me at bedtimes, too. He never failed to make me smile, acting out certain scenes in an overly-dramatic fashion, doing all the different voices and ad-libbing here and there. He made me laugh until I was clutching at my sides, tears rolling down my cheeks. In the mornings, he would drizzle an 'H' for Hermione in golden syrup on top of my porridge. "Calling all witches and wizards," he'd shout up the stairs. "It's breakfast time!"

On days when I was worried or scared about something, I imagined how Hermione would deal with it. I knew she would never let something as irrelevant as anxiety stop her. Whenever I had a lesson to go to that I hated or was bad at, I pretended I was Hermione Granger, top of the class, and walked in with my head held high. Hermione got me through my most difficult days.

Rachel loved Harry Potter, too. We'd write our own spinoff stories and act out our favourite scenes together, but I'd always make her play Harry or Ron, even though she had Hermione's curly brown hair. I hoped she didn't mind.

When the first Harry Potter film finally came out, I fell madly in love with Emma Watson. I covered my wardrobe doors with my favourite posters of her, tearing them out of magazines and newspapers, begging my mum to bring home any articles she found that had interviews with Emma in them. I remember thinking to myself that she was beautiful and wishing that I could look like her. At the time, I wasn't aware that my feelings for her might be more than admiration or envy.

I begged my parents to buy me some Gryffindor robes (I've since accepted that I'm more of a Hufflepuff) and fashioned a wand out of some twigs I found in the garden. Then, after saving up my pocket money for weeks on end, I bought some curly brown twine from the local garden centre. Armed with a pair of scissors and some Sellotape, I sat on the rug in my bedroom and carefully constructed an extravagant, multi-layered Hermione wig. I walked around town with it wrapped into my ponytail, swishing it proudly. I didn't care that people laughed. I was Hermione Granger, and I could conquer the world.

BEGINNING TO SHINE

4

A few months before I turned twelve, I made a big decision. While everyone else in my class had chosen to go to the local secondary school, I decided to go to a different one. I would know absolutely nobody, but I had very little to lose – I had been so unhappy at primary school. Little did I know at the time, it would be the best leap of faith I ever took.

Just make friends. You have to make at least one, I thought to myself as I walked through the double doors on my first day.

I was petrified. As I entered the main hall, all I could see was a mass of other Year 7s in matching navy-blue school sweatshirts, babbling excitedly.

The hall, although quite big, had a cosy feel to it. Giant, oversized curtains hung majestically over the main stage, with the school crest placed proudly above it. The smell of freshly cooked food wafted in from the canteen.

I fiddled nervously with the bottom of my sweatshirt as I walked through the crowd, looking for a place to sit. I was getting more and more anxious with each passing minute. Everyone was in groups, chatting and getting to know each other.

My heart sank and a lump rose in my throat. I stood in the corner, biting my lip, not knowing what to do.

"Hello! What's your name?" a voice from behind me asked.

I turned around and recognized Mr Nelson, the Head of Year. He was balding, with kind eyes and a knack for making people feel instantly at ease.

"I'm Lucy. Lucy Sutcliffe," I whispered hoarsely, not even trying to hide my building anxiety.

"Ah!" said Mr Nelson brightly. "You're from

outside of our school's catchment area. A newbie! Let me take you to meet the other girls who also came from different schools."

He took me firmly by the arm and led me to the other side of the room, where a group of three girls were sat in a circle on the floor – a small, dark-haired girl with a bright pink bag, a pale girl with vivid orange hair, and a taller, black-haired girl with a wide smile.

"This is Sophie, Kristine and Rebecca," he said. "Kristine has come all the way from the Philippines! Sophie and Rebecca are from primary schools in Oxford, so they don't know anybody else, either. You four are the bravest ones, coming here by yourselves – but don't tell the rest of your year group that I said that." He winked, then turned away with a cheery wave.

The three girls stared at me as I sat down. "I'm Lucy," I offered up, trying to be brave, swallowing the lump in my throat and placing my rucksack on the floor beside me.

"Nice to meet you," said Kristine, offering her

hand with a huge grin. I couldn't help but smile at the formality of the gesture. She saw me smiling and laughed. "In the Philippines, we greet everyone with a nice, firm handshake. It's tradition!" She beamed, clearly amused by the incredulous looks on our faces. I shook her hand, chuckling.

"I'm Rebecca, but you can call me Becci," whispered the smaller girl sat next to Kristine.

I noticed Becci's pencil case peeking out of her bag; it was bright pink with little photos of guinea pigs printed all over it. "Nice to meet you – I love your pencil case!" I exclaimed, pointing to her bag. "I have two guinea pigs at home, they're so cute."

Becci's face lit up. "Me too!"

"I have a dog, does that count?!" said the girl with bright orange hair. "I'm Sophie by the way!"

"No, I don't think dogs count," said Kristine seriously, trying not to laugh. Then her bottom lip began to twitch into a smile and we dissolved into giggles.

I got a sudden, almost overwhelming feeling of relief. *This is way easier than I anticipated*, I thought.

I felt like an entirely different person as I walked out of the school gates that day. Being thrust into a new environment where I was suddenly supported and liked by my peers made me realize that I had no reason to be anyone but myself. I loved what it felt like to be included and involved, without fear of being mocked or laughed at. My shy, timid personality was fading away, and a better, more confident me was appearing. I raised my hand more often and spoke up in debates and discussions. Slowly but surely, a part of me that had never been able to shine before – I liked to think of it as my inner Hermione – was beginning to emerge.

UGLY

Year 8 rolled around, and slowly, things started to change. The teachers announced that we were being divided up in terms of our abilities rather than having all of our lessons as a tutor group. I tried not to panic at the thought of having a class without anyone I knew. The happy little bubble that I'd built for myself was threatening to burst.

After checking my timetable, I was relieved to see that the only class I'd be away from my friends for was Design & Technology. But I hadn't had much of a chance to get to know the rest of the kids in my year group, and I began to get a nagging, anxious feeling that I just couldn't shake. Would I be able to make new friends?

As I walked into the classroom for my first D&T lesson, I felt like I was going to be sick – I'd never been so nervous. I sat down at a table and watched everyone else file in. I recognized a few faces that I couldn't put a name to, but no one said anything to me and I was too scared to start a conversation. I felt useless and self-conscious, and the most frustrating part was, I couldn't figure out why. *Calm down*, I repeated to myself, over and over. *You have nothing to be nervous about.*

An eccentric-looking man strolled in, holding a huge cardboard box. He had a thick, curly beard, a bright green shirt and a striped yellow tie. He looked around excitedly.

"Today, we're going to be making our product displays," he announced, handing out huge pieces of polystyrene and Stanley knives. "They'll need to be designed on the computer using a special and very complicated program, which I'll explain how to use in a bit."

The class tittered. I started to relax – perhaps

this wasn't going to be as bad as I'd thought.

Mr Stevenson turned to face the whiteboard and began to draw. "First, though, we're going to make some 3D—"

The door of the classroom crashed open. Two boys traipsed in, one swigging from a giant bottle of Irn Bru, the other scoffing a packet of crisps.

"You're late," Mr Stevenson said with a sigh, not even turning around. It seemed he had already resigned himself to what was about to happen.

The two boys looked at each other and sniggered.

"Can you find somewhere to sit, boys? You're disrupting my lesson."

The smaller boy shrugged and headed over to sit in one of two empty seats at my table. The taller one hesitated. Mr Stevenson stared at him. "Colin? Colin, sit down, please, we need to get started."

Colin shrivelled up his nose. "There's nowhere to sit. Duncan took the last seat."

The smaller boy laughed, stretching out in the

chair with a big, over-exaggerated yawn.

"There's a seat next to Duncan," Mr Stevenson gestured to the seat opposite me, exasperated. "Just sit down."

"Yeah, but I don't want to sit near her. She's ugly." He pointed at me and began to make retching noises. "She probably smells, too."

My cheeks flushed scarlet. A few people giggled nervously, but most of the room remained silent.

Mr Stevenson folded his arms and glared at Colin. "Sit down, or I'm sending you out," he snapped.

"Send me out then. I'd rather sit outside than next to her. I mean, look at her! Look at her glasses!" Colin chortled. He grabbed a Stanley knife from the nearest table and started twirling it casually around in his hands.

"Get out," said Mr Stevenson quietly.

Colin threw his empty Irn Bru bottle at the wall and sauntered out of the room, laughing loudly. Everyone was staring at me.

I told myself that I'd been called ugly

before and that it was no big deal. I told myself I could handle it – Colin was just some stupid child who knew nothing about anything. I told myself it was going to be OK, and that I wasn't *that* ugly . . . but from that moment on, I dreaded every D&T lesson. The second I set foot in the classroom, my anxiety would swell like a balloon inside my chest. And although no one in my class ever said anything, I was certain that they remembered what Colin had said and were secretly judging me.

What I didn't know was that my anxious feelings were just a taster of what was to come in my later teens. I'd developed a certain way of thinking that would eventually become a full-blown anxiety disorder that would take years of self-awareness training to reverse. But, then again, I was only twelve. What did I know?

HE'S NOT REALLY MY TYPE...

"So, I heard David really fancies you," Sophie whispered excitedly as I met her at the school gates one sunny Tuesday morning at end of the summer term. We'd just turned thirteen, and Sophie was becoming increasingly boy crazy.

"Oh!" I said, shifting my bag strap on to my left shoulder nervously, trying to sound delighted. "That's sweet."

Boys hadn't really crossed my mind since starting secondary school. Most of the boys I knew seemed nice enough (besides Colin, Duncan and a couple of other morons I'd had the misfortune of meeting), but none of them really interested me – and the feeling had been mutual, or so I'd thought. We just sort of coexisted, and that was the way I liked it.

"So, what do you think?" Sophie asked as we climbed the steps to our classroom. "Do you like him?"

I was taken aback. "He's not really my type," I found myself saying, before the thought had even been processed by my brain. I paused. I'd never properly thought about who my 'type' would be. And if David wasn't it, then who was?

As we entered our form room, I looked around at the boys in my class, sizing them up. *John is kind of cute, I suppose. He seems friendly, always chatting with everyone. And I suppose Tim is all right...*

My train of thought was interrupted by Sophie. "Lucy! LUCY! Look!"

I looked dutifully in the direction she was pointing. Our classroom door had been propped open to keep the room cool, and across the hallway, in the classroom opposite, we could see David, leaning back in his chair with his legs propped up on the table. He was staring at me.

"He, like, can't take his eyes off you," gushed Sophie with a giggle.

David winked. I smiled awkwardly and turned away.

"Oh my gosh, you totally like him back!" Sophie insisted. "You're sooo blushing!"

I was flattered, but that was where my feelings ended. I hardly knew the guy, but my hesitation only seemed to encourage Sophie's persistence, so when he asked me out during second period, I said yes just to shut her up.

At break time, I was the talk of the playing field.

"Lucy, are you going out with David?" girls in my year whom I'd never even spoken to before were asking me, incredulously.

I tried to convince myself that I liked David back. After all, there seemed no reason not to. Still – I couldn't shake the unpleasant sinking feeling in the pit of my stomach.

Just before the end of break, David came up behind me and without a word wrapped his arms around my waist. I held his sticky hands awkwardly.

I felt almost nauseous.

I stood there in his uncomfortable embrace for what felt like hours. I was so relieved when the bell finally rang that I scurried off to my French lesson without so much as a "see you later."

As I sat down, I was greeted with a flurry of questions.

"Did you kiss?!" Becci squeaked excitedly.

"No. . ." I stuttered. "It . . . it feels a bit weird with him, guys."

There was a long pause. "Do you want me to break up with him for you?" Becci said, sympathetically.

Inwardly, I breathed a quiet sigh of relief. "Um . . . yeah, yeah . . . perhaps that's for the best," I agreed, trying not to sound too keen. I wanted to hug her.

"Maybe he's just not the right guy for you," Sophie mused. "You'll find someone better!"

I looked down at my shoes. Someone better? I'd never fancied a boy. While my friends drooled over posters of movie stars like Zac Efron and Leonardo

DiCaprio, I preferred posters of Emma Watson or Cheryl from Girls Aloud. When I watched films, I was always far more interested in the female actresses. *It's because they're just inspiring women, that's all*, I thought to myself, putting the thought firmly to the back of my mind.

Later that week, David asked out Sophie and she said yes. It was the talk of the year group, and everyone wanted to know how I felt. As I was getting on my school bus one afternoon, Kristine came rushing up behind me.

"Lucy! Are you OK after what's happened?"

"After what happened?"

"You know, the whole David and Sophie thing?"

"Oh, that! Yeah, I'm fine," I said, with what I thought was a suitably pained expression. "I think," I added after a pause, worried that I didn't sound sad enough.

"But I mean ... aren't you kind of mad at her? Like, whatever happened to Girl Code, you know? Don't ever date your friend's exes, it's like, rule number one."

"Um, yeah, I guess," I lied. "But as long as they're happy, right?"

"I suppose," said Kristine. "Hope you're OK though."

"I'm sure I will be!" I said, with a little too much vigour.

Kristine patted me on the back with a sympathetic smile. "Plenty more boys out there!"

Or girls, the tiny voice in my head whispered.

DENIAL

Things can change so fast when you're not paying attention. One minute, I had been eleven years old and sitting in my maths classroom, giggling and passing notes to my friends; the next, I was fifteen and worrying about exams, my weight and why on earth I wasn't crushing on boys the way my friends were.

Sophie had made friends with another group of girls, and at the end of that year, she moved to France with her family. Kristine had also left to go to a different school, which left just Becci and me. Over the last year, the two of us had quickly become brilliant friends. She was extremely supportive and fiercely loyal. When it came to talking to her about my problems or wanting advice, I knew I could trust her with anything.

We'd recently befriended two girls named Emily and Kat, who were in our English class. The four of us got along like a house on fire. Emily lived just down the road from me and we had started hanging out a lot.

I secretly wanted to be just like Emily. She was pretty in that effortless sort of way, with big, curly eyelashes, huge blue eyes and a wardrobe full of clothes to die for. She also had a giant make-up collection, which I envied from afar. I had always been fascinated with make-up; the little glass bottles and vials in my mother's beauty cabinet reminded me of a potions class at Hogwarts.

One lunchtime, Emily offered to do my make-up for me. She lined my eyes with a fancy-looking brush and winged it out into a cat flick to look just like hers, then coloured in my lips with a bright red lip pencil. When I looked in the mirror, I was amazed. Was that really *me*?!

That evening, I rushed home and rifled through the little box of cosmetics I kept on my windowsill. Most of the things in there were little eye-shadow freebies from magazines, or bits and pieces my mum had given me that she never used. I sighed. The bright pink tubes of bubblegum-flavoured lip gloss and pots of gloopy, floral-scented body glitter were no longer right for a fifteen-year-old. I needed to take a more 'grown up' approach, so after taking a peek into my mum's make-up bag and snaffling a few select items, I began experimenting.

One afternoon after school, my mum caught sight of me as she walked through the front door. "Sweetheart," she said, trying to keep a straight face. "What is that orange stain across your forehead?"

I rubbed at it nervously. "Foundation! Why?"

"Oh, darling, I ... I don't think it's quite your shade!"

I ran to the nearest mirror and peered at my

reflection. A bright orange streak spanned across the length of my forehead. "Oh . . . oh, wow. . . !"

My mum burst out laughing. I tried to act offended, but her laugh was so infectious that soon enough, I was cackling, too.

"Did I really go to school like this?!" I said breathlessly between fits of giggles. "I look like a stripy Oompa Loompa!"

We sat down with cups of tea and chatted about make-up. At fifteen, my mum told me, the way I looked was not something I should be worrying about.

"I want people to think I'm pretty, though."

"Sweetheart, you're beautiful just the way you are. You don't need to wear make-up *at all*. Make-up is for older people like me. But if you really want to wear it, you need to wear it because *you* want to – not because someone else has told you to."

"OK then. How about I just wear some mascara?"

She paused. "Fine, if it makes you happy. But let me show you how to use it first!"

The next day, I walked into school with my freshly curled, mascara-d eyelashes.

Kat saw my face and grinned. "Aw, you look really pretty today!" I grinned. Kat was always able to put a huge smile on my face.

Emily nodded. "You really do! Trying to catch the attention of some *boys*, perhaps?!" she joked.

I laughed. Emily and Kat had a lot of guy friends, and I couldn't help envying the attention they got. On the one hand, I wanted nothing to do with boys, but at the same time, they made it all seem so cool and exciting. They were always deciphering texts from guys together and talking about their crushes in hushed whispers. It seemed sort of exhilarating. All at once, I was jealous, and found myself wanting to be a part of the action.

Now that I have a new look, maybe I can finally capture the hearts of some boys?! I thought to myself, optimistic as ever.

Sadly, my newfound confidence was short-lived. That afternoon, as I was getting off the school bus, Lewis Price, who was in the year above, came sauntering up to me. He wore a look of pure disgust. He stopped, and looked me up and down.

"What happened to *you*?"

I stared at him, confused, but didn't say anything. I tried to step around him but he stopped right in front of me.

"You look like you live in a bin."

All of his friends started to laugh. His brother William chipped in. "It's true. I'm pretty sure you get uglier and uglier every single day."

I swallowed and kept on walking, trying to hold back tears. I could hear them jeering at me as I rounded the corner.

I went home and stared in the mirror. What was wrong with the way I looked? My eyes were a bit big and my mouth was a bit small, but it was nothing too horrendous. I frowned. I suppose my teeth were a bit crooked. Should I get that looked at?

I poked and prodded at my face for hours that evening, picking apart every last detail. Emily and Kat had said I looked really pretty, but Lewis and William had said the complete opposite. So who was right? Which of them should I believe?

I wish I'd known back then that beauty is in the eye of the beholder. You can look like a supermodel and still not everyone is going to think you're beautiful. It took me a long time to realize that what is on the inside – my kindness, my loyalty, my ability to make people laugh, my passions, my dreams – is what truly counts. My mum was right: when you get ready in the morning it should be for no one else but yourself. If *you're* happy, nothing else should matter.

I'LL FANCY HIM IN NO TIME!

8

I was starting to really worry about why I still wasn't having any crushes on boys. There were guys in my year who made girls practically fall over themselves with excitement whenever they slouched by, hitching up their low-rise jeans, flicking their shaggy hair out of their eyes, guitars slung meaningfully over their shoulders. I tried to convince myself that I was just being super picky.

One evening, out of pure frustration, I tore down the posters of Emma Watson that I had plastered all over my wardrobe door and replaced them with some pictures of Zac Efron that I'd ripped out from my magazines. I gazed at them hopefully. "Wow, he's so hot," I said aloud, with a half-hearted attempt at a love-struck sigh. I felt nothing. I looked ruefully at the pile of Emma posters on the floor. What was this going to take?

Exasperated, and becoming increasingly desperate, I began scouting around for someone to have a crush on. What boys did I know? Who could I fancy?

One afternoon during English class, I spotted the perfect candidate.

Harry had green eyes, curly hair, and seemed a little arrogant – but arrogance was, according to the magazines I'd been reading, an indicator of secret insecurity. "So adorable," I thought to myself. "We can totally be insecure together."

Halfway through the lesson, Harry turned to me and asked if he could borrow a pen. I handed him the one I'd been using without a second thought, then realized I didn't have a spare. Once he'd turned back around, I asked Kat if I could borrow hers.

She began to chuckle as she reached into her

pencil case. "You've gone so red!" she whispered. "Why on earth did you give him your pen?!"

"Boys make me do stupid things, I guess," I said with a nonchalant sigh.

"You're not alone there," Emily whispered. "He asked me what my name was the other day and I temporarily forgot it!"

We fell about laughing.

"Girls! Be quiet," Mrs Fitzgerald shouted from across the room. Harry turned around and waggled his finger at us.

"I think I fancy him," I whispered.

"Me too!" Emily squeaked.

I felt as light as air as I walked home that evening. "This isn't too difficult," I thought to myself as I ambled up the garden path. "I'll fancy him in no time!"

FITTING IN

I had convinced myself: I liked Harry.

I drew his initials in heart shapes on the front of my planner, my English textbooks, and my diary. I gossiped about him with my friends, and came up with long, complex ways of getting him to fall head-over-heels in love with me. Becci, Emily, Kat and I played endless games of M.A.S.H., trying to figure out the names of our future children (Brian, Robert and Amelia) what our house was going to be like (a caravan – not my first choice, but I knew we could make it work), and what car we would drive (a VW Beetle – my favourite – it was destiny).

But it was becoming increasingly clear that Emily

had a big crush on Harry, too. I hadn't expected him to become such an integral part of our lives, and it was starting to worry me. We would spend hours talking about Harry at break times, analysing his every word, trying to decide if he had a crush on either of us. What would happen if he did? Would it ruin our friendship with each other?

Harry was loving it. He sat at our table in English and basked in the attention, our coy remarks going back and forth like a ping-pong game as we got steadily more flirtatious.

One day, Harry reached for my hand underneath the table and held it for the rest of the lesson. *This is it*, I thought. *He's totally in love with me.* But I didn't get that surge of butterflies like all the magazines had told me to expect. At the end of class, he stared at me from underneath his floppy fringe and I just looked at the floor.

So now what? I'd been so caught up in trying to like him, and getting him to like me, that I hadn't considered what would happen next. Should I ask him out?

I couldn't sleep that night. My thoughts were whirling around and around in my head. What had I done? What had I started? It had never been in my nature to compete for anything, let alone a person. I felt horrendous. I'd planned out our whole lives together in my head, but now it had actually come down to it, I didn't know what to do. Did I really like him as much as I thought? Did I actually want to go ahead and *date* him?

Deep down, I knew the answer was no. Guilt washed over me in waves. What would Emily think? She genuinely liked him, and I felt sick at the thought that I might have taken him away from her.

Over the next few weeks, Harry seemed more subdued than usual. He didn't sit at our table in English, and he didn't speak to either Emily or me. Emily seemed like her normal self, talking and gossiping like nothing was wrong – but I could feel the tension mounting between the three of us. I just wanted it all to fade away. Why had my feelings changed so abruptly? What was wrong with me? I felt so guilty. This was all my fault.

My saving grace came at the end of the week in the form of a geography field trip to Swansea. I wasn't going, but Harry, Emily and Kat were. I wondered what was going to happen while they were away. I secretly hoped that Emily had magically guessed that I wasn't into Harry any more. I didn't want to have to tell her. I didn't want to look like a liar.

When they came back five days later, rumours began to fly that Emily and Harry were now an item. Kat confirmed the news to me during break time. She spoke gently and quietly, as if she thought I was going to cry at any minute.

"It's cool," I said, and I meant it. "I don't mind. They're better suited to each other."

It wasn't long before Emily came to speak to me, too. One look at her worried face made me feel guilty all over again.

"You're one of my closest friends now," she said, "and . . . I just want to make sure you aren't mad at me or anything."

"Of course not! I promise it's OK."

"Pinkie swear?"

"Pinkie swear!"

We both laughed.

As much as I'd felt like my crush on Harry had been real, I also knew deep down that when I'd told Emily and Kat that I didn't mind, I was telling the truth. I didn't care that Harry had chosen her – and it terrified me.

Sport had never been my strong point, and PE lessons were just as drab at secondary school as they had been at primary school. Now, though, it was a chance to hang out and catch up with friends that we didn't share other classes with. As long as we at least *pretended* to exercise, none of our teachers seemed to care that we spent most of the lesson gossiping.

Half an hour into one particularly gruelling cross-country running lesson, I was ambling along by myself, stopping every so often to smell the flowers, when I spotted my friend Clare walking ahead of me with Nathan, who I knew from maths class, and another girl that I didn't recognize.

I jogged up to them and tapped Clare on the shoulder.

She turned around, smiling. "Oh, hello! This is Bel, by the way."

Bel smiled at me nervously. "Hi!"

I smiled back. "I like how all four of us have just given up on running."

The three of them laughed. "I'm so glad I found people who hate PE as much as I do," Bel said, grinning.

"Oh God, tell me about it," Nathan said. "I dread these lessons."

I did an impression of our PE teacher Miss Bernard, running on the spot looking constipated. I wasn't looking where I was going, and got my foot stuck in a large dollop of cow poo. I slipped over spectacularly, and landed on the floor in a heap.

"Clare," I said, looking up at her, trying to keep a straight face. "Could you clean up after yourself next time?"

We were in stiches, guffawing all the way up the lane.

"Oh dear," said Bel, wiping tears of mirth from her eyes. "I'm always going to remember this. Meeting you for the first time, resulting in you stepping into poo."

That set us off again. I had a feeling Bel and I were going to be best friends.

Once again, it struck me how lucky I was to have such a brilliant circle of friends. We had become a really tight-knit group. The six of us – Emily, Becci, Kat, Bel, Clare and I – hung out after school and at the weekends, getting together to eat pizza, listen to music and gossip. It felt good to have a group of people in my life that I had so much in common with and could really trust. I thought back to how lonely and friendless I'd felt when I was eleven. If only I'd known how much happiness was to come.

Still, though, there was something missing. Something important.

A LIFE WITHOUT LOVE?

11

I was almost sixteen. I had wonderful friends. I had a loving family. But there was one thing I would never have: love.

That was the conclusion I had come to. If I couldn't fall in love with boys like Harry or Zac Efron, then I quite clearly wasn't going to fall in love with anyone. My destiny, it seemed, was to remain "neutral"; I would live in a secluded log cabin on a farm somewhere, breed dogs maybe, and grow my own food in a tiny vegetable patch. I would star-gaze and learn new languages and watch the flowers grow. I would live life to its fullest – but I would absolutely not fall in love.

Just writing about this time makes my heart ache. I was so utterly wrapped up in a twisted game of doubt and self-loathing that I willingly accepted a life devoid of love if it meant that I could keep my worrying lack of feelings for boys hidden for ever.

What made things worse was that I couldn't tell anyone. They say a problem shared is a problem halved, but I had to carry my burden alone. I desperately wanted to tell my parents, or one of my friends – deep down, I knew they'd all love me no matter what – but something was keeping me silent. What if they got angry at me for lying to them? Would they be disappointed, or worse, *embarrassed*, by me? If I told one person, would everyone eventually find out? Would it become the talk of the town? The last thing I wanted was to be defined by this one "part" of my character – especially when I was still trying to figure out what that "part" was. And what if news broke out before I was ready? I couldn't risk that. . .

I knew my worries were irrational, but the

isolation I'd put myself in only heightened my anxiety, and gradually, I sank deeper and deeper into a whirlwind of confusion and misery. While days spent with my friends were full of fun and laughter, as soon as I was on my own, my mind became a tightly wound spiral of panic. I obsessively analysed every passing thought, searching for an answer, desperate for a clue, scouring for anything that might help curb the swelling terror inside my head. I felt anxious and sick every single day. Sometimes my chest felt so tight that I was certain I was having a heart attack. I couldn't concentrate on anything but my own thoughts.

I couldn't sleep. Night after night I cried into my pillow as the small hours ticked by, kept awake by the chaotic thoughts in my brain. Was it just a phase? Was I *gay* or something? It was the first time I had used this label, even tentatively. How would I ever really know? What was going to happen if I told somebody?

I cried so much that my face felt sore

from all the salt in my tears. To soothe my aching skin, I'd stand at my window with it thrust wide open, lights off, staring up into the starry night sky. They'd always be there, sparkling away, a distant twinkle high up above the dark village horizon – my silent beacons of hope. The nagging voice in my head would be drowned out by the wind as it whistled through my room, rustling my curtains, rattling the posters on my walls, tousling my hair. "There, there," it would whisper, softly. At last I would feel at peace, somehow soothed by the way nature never stops, refusing to slow down for anyone, or anything.

I was at my most calm just before dawn. As the sun would rise in the east, the sky would turn a soft magenta, and the rooftops, once shrouded in darkness, became navy silhouettes against the fiery glow. At this point, I would collapse into bed, exhausted. In those rare, blissful moments, I dared to think ahead, about my future, my prospects, and my goals. Sometimes I saw myself, aged 25, happy and successful, maybe married with kids, living with someone I loved. A man? A woman? The scene was too vague for me to know. These moments in which I allowed my mind to wander were the ones that pushed me forwards through my darkest days. Those few minutes of peace became what I lived for.

A CRUSH

12

Despite everything, my dreams of living a loveless life alone in the mountains were short-lived. That's the thing about love: you never know when it's about to hit you smack bang in the face.

When I say love, I of course use the term loosely. I was sixteen and I had a crush. But, boy, did I have a crush with all my might.

Melissa Edwards was fascinating in all the ways Harry hadn't been. She was beautiful, endearing and smart. When she laughed, she lit up the whole room. My year group was so big that I'd never seen her before, but she'd been put in several of my new classes and the first time she made eye contact with me, I turned red and went weak at the knees. I smiled, desperately wanting to look calm and collected, then ducked behind my textbook trying to hide my embarrassment and the uncontrollable grin that had spread itself across my face. My heart was beating so fast, I could feel it in my ears.

I went home that evening and practised my best "casual smile" in the mirror. I flicked my hair around in what I hoped was an effortless and confident sort of way. Next time I saw her, I would keep my cool – no blushing, no hiding behind textbooks.

The very next day, she spotted me in the corridor on her way out of school. It was the end of fifth period and kids were beginning to spill out of classrooms in their hordes. My heart was in my mouth. As I joined the throng of people, she smiled at me from across the hallway.

"Hiya!"

I suddenly forgot every single word in the English language. In that split second, my brain put two and two together and got five.

"Bye-a!"

She laughed and kept on walking. I wanted to disappear.

What the hell, Lucy? I thought angrily as I stomped towards the school gates. *Bye-a? Like "bye" because you were leaving, but also "hiya" because that's what she said to you, right? Nice one, brain. God, I'm such an idiot!*

Melissa didn't seem too bothered by my spluttering display though, and over the weeks that followed, I finally got the hang of speaking coherent sentences to her.

One afternoon, sitting across the table from me during an endless science lesson, she caught me mid-yawn. "Hey, Lucy, do you know what our homework was? I wasn't listening!"

"I don't know, but I hope it involves sleeping," I said, finishing my yawn with a grin.

She threw her head back, laughing hysterically, clapping her hands with delight.

"I WISH!" she screeched.

I spent the rest of the day on cloud nine.

I began to notice that the way Melissa made me feel had temporarily silenced the negative thoughts that had been swirling around my brain. I quietly admitted to myself that the way I felt about her was far more sincere than any feelings I'd ever had for David or Harry. And while I was half-convinced that she was a one-off, I was able to be more honest with myself than I had been in years. This was a turning point in my journey to self-acceptance.

I went home one evening to find Melissa had added me on Facebook. I told myself to wait a few hours before accepting the friend request so I didn't look too keen, but I only lasted fifteen minutes before my excitement got the better of me. I clicked "accept," and almost immediately, a notification popped up in my newsfeed:

"Melissa is in a relationship."

My heart sank as I stared at the screen. Was this a coincidence, or was it just the world's way of telling me that she and I were never going to happen? The heavy weight of disappointment hit me like a train. I had always known deep down that nothing was going to come of this – after all, I'd never considered actually acting on the way I felt – but that hadn't stopped me from dreaming about it.

Slowly, my feelings for her began to fade. We still spoke occasionally, and it was nice to be able to converse without my face flushing crimson, but gradually, I stopped thinking about her. At the end of Year 10, she was transferred to a different class and soon she became just another face in the crowd.

But I had found myself at a crossroads. The possibility that I was gay was not something I could ignore any more. It was no longer the tiny whisper of a thought which reared its ugly head at night-time; it was a wailing, flashing siren with bright white lights and signs pointing to it. And so, reluctantly, I accepted the possibility. I *might* be, I told myself. I *could* be. And all at once, I became intrigued by my feelings instead of being scared of them.

LABELS

13

I decided things would be easier to process if I found some sort of label for myself. In my head, having a label meant fitting into a category – and fitting into a category was something I desperately needed in that moment. I wanted to feel like I was a part of something. I wanted to know what it felt like to be included.

I didn't know anyone who wasn't straight. The whole concept of being something "else" felt foreign and alien to me – like something I should be learning about in some indie film or TV show. It didn't feel like it should be so close to home, let alone something that might apply to *me*. Was

I jumping the gun a little? I thought back to how Melissa had made me feel. *You need to figure this out*, said the voice in my head.

One evening, while my family was getting ready for bed, I went into my bedroom, shut the door and switched on my computer. Checking behind me every few seconds, I googled the word "sexuality" and clicked through to a website that claimed it would help "define" me with a short quiz. Nervously, I clicked through the questions, worried that someone was going to knock on my door at any minute. The page reloaded and a photo of a woman holding a flashing sign popped up:

"You are most likely to be a) gay or b) bisexual!"

I stared at the screen. Gay? I swallowed, heart pounding. I didn't want to think about it. But bisexual? That could work. This way, I would have the best of both worlds! I felt like I'd discovered some kind of loophole. It was like I'd made a compromise with myself – I could be one thing, as long as I was another, too.

I'm certain now that trying to put a label on

myself at sixteen was one of the worst things I could have done – especially when the label came from a five-question quiz on some dodgy website. Labels can put such an unnecessary amount of pressure on people who are still unsure about who they are. It can be damaging to try and fit yourself into a category when you're still growing and changing. What it all comes down to is what *you're* most comfortable with. It's about finding out what works best for *you,* rather than listening to anyone who tries to tell you what you can and can't be.

So I began calling myself bisexual – but only inside my own head. I still hadn't told anyone, and I wasn't planning to any time soon. I still felt sick at the thought of telling my friends and family. There was no way I was going to mention it to them. The fear of being laughed at, made fun of, or doubted, kept my mouth shut, even though I knew deep down that none of them would even dream of doing that.

I wasn't ready.

SECRETS

14

"So..." whispered Emily in hushed, dramatic tones. "Anyone got any new crushes?"

We were at my house having a sleepover, and Emily, Kat, Bel, Becci and Clare were all squeezed into my kitchen. We had come down for some snacks as the clock neared midnight and we'd ended up building a huge den, scattering cushions on the floor and hanging sheets up from the ceiling light fixtures. It felt like we were five years old again, sitting cross-legged on the floor under a canopy of blankets, eating crisps and cupcakes, giggling.

Sipping on her hot chocolate, Emily leant further in to the circle. "No big, juicy secrets?"

My heart stopped.

"Nope," sighed Bel. "Does that make me boring?"

Everyone laughed. Bel was pretty outspoken – if she'd had any juicy secrets, we'd have known about them by now.

"We need gossip!" Becci joked with a grin. She was one of the quieter girls in the group, but she loved intrigue as much as any of us.

"My life is an open book," Clare said. "If that makes me boring, I don't care!"

"Me too," I said, suddenly. I felt panicked, like I'd been caught in a spotlight off guard. "I don't have any secrets."

Kat nodded. "Keeping secrets from you guys would be too hard, anyway. I'd never be able to keep them to myself!"

For the rest of the evening, I felt guilty. My friends and I were such a close group and here I was, lying straight to their faces. I knew that they'd love me no matter what, but try as I might, I couldn't bring myself to tell them the truth. Whenever the conversation steered back to boys, I tried to think of something to say. Should I just come out with it? Or was now not the right time? I couldn't shake the nagging feeling in the pit of my stomach. I felt isolated and alone, with my deepest darkest secret getting closer to my heart and further from my mouth with every passing day. I couldn't do it. I couldn't tell them. I didn't want anyone to know.

As the hands of the clock approached 4 a.m. and my friends began to drift off to sleep, I stared up at the ceiling of blankets, trying not to cry.

THE L WORD

15

Hope tends to rear its glittering head when you least expect it to.

One morning, during a particularly tedious maths lesson, I was scrolling absent-mindedly through Tumblr and came across a post from someone about a television show called *The L Word*. *"There is no other TV show quite like this one,"* the person had written. Intrigued, I googled *The L Word* and read the Wikipedia synopsis:

"The L Word is a television drama series which portrays the lives of a group of lesbian, bisexual,

straight and transgender people in the trendy
Los Angeles area of California."

I was taken aback. I'd seen gay people on television before – I loved Alan Carr's chat shows, and sometimes watched Sue Perkins and Stephen Fry on *QI* – but being gay was never something I'd heard them talk about. Not in any depth anyway. I'd never seen an entire series dedicated to the concept of sexuality – especially based around a circle of women who were just like me. It was unheard of. I had to see this for myself.

Over the next two months, once everyone else in my family had gone to sleep, I would creep over to my computer, plug my headphones in, and load up *The L Word*. I was enthralled. When the characters cried, I cried. When they laughed, I laughed. I became utterly invested in their storylines. They were like the gay best friends I never had. I felt suddenly connected, and more importantly, I felt at ease. Here was a group of women, living ordinary, happy, successful lives, while embracing their sexualities. Through this show that I'd happened upon just by chance, I was suddenly learning about things like equality, women's rights, and feminism. My mind had been blown – I didn't know half of these concepts even existed. There was so much to take in, but I was desperate to fill in the gaps.

The L Word had opened my eyes. It completely changed my outlook on my life, my identity, and my sexuality. I was sixteen and just as confused as ever, but a sort of quiet hopefulness had taken root within me. Some day I knew I would have the courage to accept myself for who I was, whatever that might be. For the first time in my life, the little voice in my head whispered, *so what?*

THE VILLAGE PLAYERS

16 ✈

Summer was coming to an end. One evening in late August, I met up with Rachel for a cycle ride. I hadn't seen her for months, but the same old camaraderie we'd always had was back in an instant. We grabbed our bicycles and headed for the fields, water bottles in hand, rucksacks slung over our shoulders.

With the evening sun beating down on our backs, we hurtled down Church Lane at top speed, whooping with delight as we swerved around corners, dodging potholes and whizzing past clusters of sleepy little cottages, their thatched roofs ablaze against the fiery orange glow of the slowly setting sun. As we neared the bottom of the hill, we came to a gradual stop, dismounted our bikes, and hid them in a nearby hedge out of sight. We went the rest of the way on foot, climbing over gates and squeezing through stiles, our flip-flops click-clacking over the scalding hot gravel as we made our way down the narrow path.

Reaching an ancient dry stone wall, we scrambled breathlessly to the top, shielding our eyes from the sun. We could see the entire village from where we stood. The hill that we'd cycled down was now just a thin black stripe in the distance, and beyond that, the main road, snaking through the vivid green hedgerows, dipping in and out of sight between the willow trees. Golden-brown fields stretched lazily out in front of us like a vast patchwork quilt, each one a slightly different colour and size. The thatched cottages we had passed were now tiny, doll's-house-sized dots, and beyond those, we could spot little speckled hay bales here and there in amongst the meadows.

We stood there for ages, taking it all in. All we could hear when the wind died down was the distant rumble of lawnmowers and the gentle pitter-patter of sprinklers on scorching hot tarmac. Then we hopped over the wall and laid our jackets out in the tall grass, opened up our rucksacks and brought out snacks: a huge tub of olives, some Pringles, a box of strawberries and a massive stick of French bread.

"We are so aggressively middle class," Rachel chuckled, opening up the olives.

The church bells began to chime as the clock struck six, and for a while, we sat in silence, munching away at our picnic, listening to the sheep bleating softly in the field next to us. The sun, now a blazing red ball in the sky, had engulfed the church spire in warm orange light, an elegant silhouette against the hushed village horizon. In moments like these, my mind was clear and my thoughts were silent. I was able to take in the world around me and bask in its awe-inspiring beauty. I felt at peace.

The conversation turned to self-esteem and

confidence. I told Rachel about how anxious I felt sometimes, and how difficult it was to be fearless when all you really wanted to do was cower in the corner.

Rachel nodded sympathetically. "That's why I joined the Village Players a few years ago," she said. "It's really helped with my confidence."

"The what?"

"The Village Players. The amateur dramatics society here in the village."

The sun started to dip behind the clouds. We began to pack up our things.

"Do they let anyone join?" I said, intrigued. "It sounds really cool, but I'm not sure I'd be good enough ... or brave enough!"

We clambered back over the wall and started up the path, heading towards the hedge where we'd left our bicycles.

"Anyone can join. And you don't have to play a main character – I mean, you can just be in the ensemble if you'd prefer. Not that you wouldn't make a fabulous Toad of Toad Hall!"

Cinderella

The next morning at school, I mentioned the Village Players to Emily.

"I want to come!" she said, excitedly.

Our friend Monkey (a self-chosen nickname), whom we'd befriended on a school trip to Berlin a couple of months back, overheard. "A theatre group?! Count me in!" He did a little twirl, which had us in stitches.

So that evening, the four of us headed back down Church Lane towards the village hall to meet the Village Players. Rachel, who had been a part of the group for years, introduced us to everyone.

I looked around the hall. Most people were much

older than us – some even in their early seventies. Besides Monkey, Emily, Rachel and me there were only a couple of other teens – a boy named Ben who I recognized from primary school, and a friend of his.

The four of us sat on the floor next to Ben and his friend, who was called Mossy. I hadn't seen Ben in years, but we quickly got chatting and started talking about our favourite books like no time had passed. He'd always been quiet and reserved at school, but he seemed to have come out of his shell a lot more since then. I'd forgotten how thoughtful and articulate he was, and listening to him speak brought a strange sense of calm over me.

I was in a new and unfamiliar environment, but I didn't feel nervous at all. I was surrounded by my friends, and I knew I was safe with them, so I was able to stop worrying about looking stupid or saying the wrong thing and instead focus on having fun.

Rachel explained that with each new production,

one of the adults in the group was given the chance to direct. This time around, it would be Ben's dad, Steve.

Steve walked in and called the whole group over. We formed a circle around him. There was a sense of anticipation and excitement in the air.

"Hello, everyone! Thanks for coming. I see we have some new faces here today!" He looked over his glasses at Monkey, Emily and me, and smiled. "Thanks for coming, guys! As you know, I've been asked to direct this season's play. And I'm pleased to announce that this time around, we'll be performing *Cinderella*!"

A handful of people clapped excitedly.

"I'm being cast as Cinderella, right?" Mossy interjected, grinning. Everyone laughed.

Steve began handing out scripts. "Unless you tell me otherwise, I'm going to assume you're all trying out for every role. If you'd rather not have a large part, please let me know."

I swallowed. I wanted to raise my hand, but I was too scared. Steve started talking about performance dates, and I zoned out instinctively. My mind was in overdrive. Should I just audition and see what happened? Surely I wouldn't be cast as a main character? I looked around nervously. There were about twenty other people in the room, most of whom had been a part of the Village Players for a while. They would be the ones getting the bigger roles, right?

The little voice in my head spoke up. *Why not aim high?* it said, softly. *You never know what might happen.*

Steve pointed at me. "I'd like you to try out for Cinderella first, please."

My heart stopped. *This is your time to shine*, said the voice in my head, a little more loudly this time. *Give it all you've got!*

My heart was beating so fast I could feel it in my ears. Everyone was looking at me. I took a deep breath, turned to page one and began to read the lines. Rachel, who was trying out for the role of the Prince, read alongside me. I reminded myself that Rachel and I had spent years goofing around, acting out the little shows that we'd written. The only difference now was that we had a real audience instead of our teddy bears.

I was starting to enjoy myself.

I could see Rachel trying to stay in character as we finished the scene. She clapped and whooped as I said my final line, and we high-fived each other from across the circle.

"Excellent!" said Steve. "A little slower next time perhaps. But great – I think that's all I need to see from you." He looked around the circle. "Who's next?"

My mind was reeling. I was on an adrenaline high, and it was only as we neared the end of the session that I realized I hadn't tried out for any other role. I looked at the clock. It was too late to say anything.

The next day, Steve emailed to say that I'd been cast as Cinderella.

Later that morning he sent out a full list of cast members, and I was pleased to see that everyone had been given a role. Rachel had been cast as the

Prince, Mossy as the Dame, Emily and Monkey as chorus members, and Ben as the "Rogue Gorilla". (Casting Ben as something weird appeared to be part of an ongoing inside joke...)

For the rest of the day, I stood a little taller. For the first time in what felt like my whole life, I was proud of myself – really, really proud.

SECOND NATURE

Rehearsals for *Cinderella* began on my seventeenth birthday. The six of us set off down Church Lane for our first full read-through, scripts in hand. As we neared the village hall, it slowly dawned on me that now I'd been given the lead, I couldn't back down. In four months' time, I would be standing on stage, performing in front of hundreds of people. I had no way out. I had to go through with it.

Old Lucy would have panicked. Old Lucy would have found some excuse to get out of it, plagued by anxiety. But New Lucy shrugged her shoulders and kept on walking. New Lucy knew that she would probably mess up a few times before she got it right, but that she'd been given this part for a reason.

People trusted me, and I wasn't going to let them down.

I didn't know where this newfound confidence had come from, but I was loving it. *Cinderella* was nothing more than a village pantomime, but being cast as the lead had completely opened my eyes. I had a responsibility to do the best I could – and it was a responsibility to myself as much as it was to the rest of the cast. Deep down, I knew I'd be OK on that stage because I'd spent my childhood pretending to be characters from books. Aged nine, when the girls in my street had run away from me, laughing, I pretended I was Hermione Granger and that I didn't care one bit. When those boys had called me ugly when I was twelve, I remembered Anne Shirley's bravery and chose to rise above it. And being cast as Cinderella was no different – I was just playing another character. It was second nature to me.

Autumn had arrived, and most nights we were

now walking to rehearsals in the dark. Church Lane, famous for its cherry blossom trees during the summertime, was unrecognizable during the colder months. One blustery evening, bundled up in our scarves, hats and coats, the six of us wandered down the hill. The trees, now completely bare, stood barren by the roadside, trunks blackened from the damp mildew, each branch standing to attention, their stark outlines jutting out against the darkening sky. As the moon rose, a heavy frost began to settle on the grassy embankments, crunching beneath our feet as we edged down the road, trying not to slip. It was quiet down there except for our excitable chatter, which came out in little puffs of condensation. Even in the darkness, the street lamps of the nearest town were enough to cast a strange orange hue over the surrounding fields, making them glitter and sparkle as the frost grew steadily thicker. Crisp, crunchy leaves lay strewn across the road, while smaller piles lay by the curb, shoved to the side by a road sweeper, left to rot in the gutter. The further we walked, the larger the piles got, until eventually we came across a pile by the verge that was nearly four feet high.

Mossy stopped. "Guys. . ."

He didn't have to say anything else. We ran towards the pile, and within seconds, leaves were flying everywhere. We rolled around in them like little kids, throwing them at each other, tossing them into the air, spinning round and round breathlessly as they fell on us like snowflakes, landing in our hair, our eyes, on our shoulders. We lay on the ground in a circle, panting as the leaves began to settle again, our ribs aching from laughter.

We arrived at the village hall fifteen minutes late, cheeks flushed, hair ragged, covered in leaves. Happy little moments that I'll remember forever.

By the time November arrived, the play was beginning to take shape. Lines had been memorized and costumes were being planned out, and one evening we managed to do the entire performance without taking a break or reading from our scripts. There was a sense of excitement in the air and a feeling of camaraderie amongst the cast. With a few short weeks before our first performance, I was confident that it would all go smoothly.

More than this, though, the play had given me something to focus on. I had a tangible goal, and it made me so happy. I was sleeping better, working harder, and was able to think more clearly. Now that I had something bigger and more important to think about, my anxiety over my sexuality had quietly taken a back seat. Life was peaceful.

Then, all of a sudden, it was opening night.

My friends and I sat backstage, perched on a couple of old sofas, going over lines one last time. I was trying to stay calm – but the atmosphere around us was manic. The hair and make-up artists were sprinting back and forth doing final touch-ups, the costume designers were adding last minute safety pins to baggy costumes, and the tech crew were trying to make sure everyone was mic'd and ready to go. I swallowed, twiddling nervously with the microphone wire taped to the inside of my dress, trying to ignore the butterflies swirling in my stomach.

As the pantomime dame, Mossy had been decked out with a giant, curly white wig, and styled by the costume designer in head to toe pink; a huge, frilly dress with a tutu, fishnet tights and massive stilettos. He was quite the spectacle.

He pursed his bright red lips in the mirror. "Wow . . . I make a really stunning woman."

I laughed, but a sudden wave of nausea hit me in the gut and I doubled over.

"Luce? Luce, are you OK?"

I ran to the bathroom, shaking, suddenly overwhelmed. My ears were ringing, I felt dizzy, and my heart was beating so hard that I could see it rising and falling in my chest. I closed my eyes and tried to focus on steadying my breathing.

A few moments later, Mossy and Emily knocked on the door of my toilet cubicle.

"Are you all right, Luce?"

I took a deep breath and stared up at the ceiling. "You're going to be OK," I told myself. "You've been rehearsing this non-stop for months. You've got this."

I opened the door. "I'm just nervous," I croaked. "Really, really nervous."

"You're gonna be fine, Lucy. I promise," said Mossy with a sympathetic smile. Emily hugged me.

As the first act started, the butterflies in my stomach grew more and more uncomfortable. I sat by the side of the stage behind the curtain, watching it all unfold. Mossy did his first scene and forgot half of his lines, but the audience were in stitches. He ambled off stage, hitching up his dress with a huge grin on his face.

"Easy crowd!" he said to me with a chuckle, squeezing my hand. "Fake it till you make it, OK?"

I heard my cue, took a deep breath, and stepped out into the spotlight. A hush fell over the audience. "She's beautiful," I heard a woman in the front row whisper.

As I began to speak, my anxiety melted away. Rachel bounded on to the stage a few minutes in and we did our first duet as Cinderella and the Prince. By the end of it, I was grinning from ear to ear. Adrenaline coursed through my veins, and as I exited stage left, I leapt into the air and into Mossy and Emily's arms.

The rest of the performance went without a

hitch. The audience laughed in all the right places, and even when the actors forgot their lines, people were so amused that they didn't seem to care.

I fell in love with the way it felt to be on stage. I thought I would hate being stared at by hundreds of people, but it was exhilarating. It was worlds away from how Colin Berk had stared at me all those years ago, disgust in his eyes, refusing to sit beside me because I was "ugly". This time around, people were looking at me in admiration, and it felt amazing. I was in control. I was safe.

At the end of the performance, the whole cast went up on stage for one final bow. The audience were going crazy, shouting and whooping as we each took our turn. Mossy did an extravagant twirl in his dress, curtseying and blowing kisses at old ladies. Everyone was laughing hysterically. As I took my bow, I looked out at the room and spotted my mum, dad and granny in the front row, beaming with pride, clapping as hard as they could.

As the curtain fell, the music started playing,

and we headed backstage. The audience were still whooping. Everyone was hugging and congratulating each other. I was on top of the world.

Ben's dad came in, clapping along to the music with a huge grin on his face.

"Great job, everyone! Especially you, Cinderella."

THE BIG DIPPER

20

I had gained a secret new skill. To add to my inner-Hermione mode, I now had an inner Cinderella-mode, too. Whenever I felt nervous, I switched it on and pretended I had the confidence of an actress. Sometimes it felt so real that I didn't even have to act.

We returned to the Village Players season after season, performing different shows. The village hall was like a second home to me, with its dusty smell, crumbling piano in the corner and sunset views from the big, wide windows. In the depths of winter we stood, shivering, sipping hot chocolate in our coats and scarves, trying to stay warm. In the height of summer, we lay out on the tiny back patio reciting lines from our wilted positions on the floor, sipping out-of-date orange squash from the kitchen fridge, fanning ourselves with our scripts.

During one rehearsal for a performance of *Aladdin*, Mossy brought his friend Chris along with him.

"I wanted to know what all the fuss was about!" Chris grinned. "I can see why you guys love this so much."

I loved the fact that I now had a group of friends who lived close to me. We self-proclaimed "village folk" hung out pretty much every weekend, as well as most evenings after school. We spent our days running through the fields, climbing trees, and sitting on hay bales drinking cider until the stars came up. Some evenings we'd head down to our local pub and sit in the garden, snacking on crisps, playing darts with the barman, and chatting with the other locals. It felt so good to be a part of something.

One evening, as we were walking back from

the pub, Ben stopped and pointed up at the sky. There, right in front of us, hung a vast, red moon – a perfect circle, glowing like an orb, casting a deep, blood-orange tinge across the sky.

"Holy cow," Chris whispered.

We stood for a minute, awestruck, looking up into the sky, completely taken in by the view.

The air was still, and utterly silent. Every now and then, a warm breeze would pick up, ruffling our hair and clothes. Then it would die down again, and we were met with a silence so profound that I could hear my own heartbeat.

We walked home as a group, and Ben, ever the gentleman, insisted on making sure the girls got home safely. Having dropped the others off, the two of us decided to take a detour back to my house, and ended up in a field at the top of Church Lane, where Rachel and I had sat all those months before.

We sat in the grass for nearly an hour, staring upwards, pointing out constellations, trying to spot planets. The sky was the clearest I had ever seen it;

thousands upon thousands of tiny twinkling lights shone down on us like fairies, basking in the eerie red glow from the low-hanging moon.

"I've always thought that that one looks like a saucepan," I said, pointing.

"That's the Big Dipper," said Ben, chuckling. "But it could totally pass as a saucepan, you're right!"

"It's the only one I'm ever able to pick out," I said, grinning. "I always look for it whenever I'm star-gazing."

"Do you star-gaze a lot?"

"Only when I'm feeling lonely."

"Me too."

We sat for a while in silence. Then Ben spoke up. "Whenever either of us are feeling lonely, we should just look for the Big Dipper. It can be our little thing! A way to stop us feeling as lonely, even if we're far apart."

I laughed, then nodded and smiled. "Deal."

A VALENTINE

21

"I'm pretty sure Mossy has a crush on you, Luce!" Chris said one evening with a wink.

I looked down at my feet, staying quiet. It was true that Mossy had started acting differently around me. He was texting me more often than usual, paying me compliments. I adored Mossy. He was one of the nicest, funniest, kindest people I had ever met. He was fiercely loyal, was always there when I wanted to chat, and was the first to make me smile again if I was feeling down. I wanted to like him back, the same way I had with Harry, only this time, it was more difficult because Mossy was, well, Mossy. I loved him as a friend – a best friend, even – but that was it. I loved him, but I wasn't *in* love with him. I knew now, more than ever, that I just *wasn't interested in boys*.

Time, I told myself. That was all that was needed. With time, his feelings would surely fade, the way mine had for Melissa. Right?

It was Valentine's Day, and I was upstairs cleaning my bedroom when I heard the sudden rattle of the letterbox. I got to the peephole just in time to see a hooded figure dressed all in black scurrying back down the path. Whoever it was clearly did not want to be seen.

A small red envelope lay on the doormat.

I picked it up and opened it, bemused. It was addressed to me. I pulled out a piece of paper and unfolded it cautiously. Then there was a tiny clink, and a delicate silver ring with the word "love" inscribed on the outside fell into my palm. My heart stopped. "Oh my goodness..."

My phone beeped, making me jump. A text from

Rachel appeared:

OH MY GOD.

What? I texted back, hurriedly.

Meet me at the top of the road, NOW!

What was going on? I rushed out of the front door and spotted Rachel speeding towards me. She looked pale and nervous, and kept looking around as if she was being watched.

"LOOK!" She sprinted up to me and thrust a piece of paper into my hands.

I scanned it. It appeared to be some kind of hand-written love poem, covering both sides of the page.

"Erm . . . what am I supposed to be looking at?"

"Look at who it's from," said Rachel, breathlessly.

I frowned and turned the page.

"Love from *BEN?!* Oh my GOD!"

"I know! A hooded figure dropped it through my letterbox just now, it must have been him. I had no idea he liked me like *that*! I don't know what to do – he's such a lovely, genuine guy, but . . . I feel like we'd be better off as friends. . ." she trailed off, helplessly. "Wait, what's that in your hand?"

I looked down and realized I was still clutching my envelope.

"Oh! It came through my letterbox just now – it's a ring!"

"WHAT! From who?!"

It suddenly occurred to me that I hadn't even read the note that came with it. I opened it with shaking hands.

"Oh my God . . . it's from Mossy!"

"Woah. Wait, hold up a second. Did that come at the same time as my letter from Ben? Do you think this was this some kind of . . . joint gesture?"

There was a long pause. We looked down at the envelopes in our hands, then back up at each other.

"He wrote me a POEM!" Rachel screeched.

"He gave me a RING!" I screeched back.

"What do we DO?" we wailed.

It turned out that it had indeed been a joint gesture. They'd been planning it for weeks, and had agreed that delivering the gifts to us on Valentine's Day, at the exact same time, while wearing matching hoods, would make it seem more mysterious and romantic. . .

The trouble was, we didn't want romance. Neither Rachel nor I saw them as anything more than friends.

We felt awful.

FOR OLD TIMES' SAKE

22

Turning Mossy down was horrible. I desperately wanted to come clean and explain how confused I'd been feeling about my sexuality, and how exhausted I was from trying to figure everything out before I tried to date anyone. In the end, though, all I could do was hug him.

"The ring is so beautiful, and it was such a sweet gesture. I just feel like, you know ... we work so well as friends. I would never want to ruin that."

"I know, Luce. I understand."

"I'll still wear the ring, though. It can be our friendship ring!"

"Promise?"

"Promise!"

I kept my word.

That night, for the first time in months, I stayed up and looked out for the Big Dipper. I quietly wondered if Ben was doing the same. I wanted so badly to have someone to talk to, someone to listen, so I could get it all out of my head. I gazed at the moon and thought about who I could confide in. Emily? Bel? The two of them would love me no matter what, I knew that. So what was holding me back?

I sighed. Fear, obviously. Fear of rejection. Fear of losing my friends and family. Fear of having to suddenly be myself, all at once, after seventeen years of hiding it all away. I started to cry. I didn't know how much longer I could wait.

Six years later, we had a little Christmas get-together at Ben's house. Emily had organized a Secret Santa, and Ben, who was dressed up in an extravagant, head-to-toe elf costume, was reading out labels and handing around presents.

"Luce – this one appears to be for you!"

He handed me a tiny little bag. I pulled the drawstring, intrigued, and out fell a beautiful silver ring, with the word "love" inscribed on the outside.

I looked up and caught Mossy's eye.

"For old times' sake," he grinned, chuckling. "Figured your other one was getting old."

I loved that it had become something we could joke about. I'd felt guilty for such a long time, but Mossy had taken it in his stride and been so understanding.

I thanked my lucky stars once again that I had such wonderful friends.

23 A CONFESSION

As it turned out, I wasn't the only one struggling with a Big Secret.

Nathan Genese was bookish and slightly geeky; the type of guy who constantly went above and beyond what was required of him in class, always going overboard with homework, determined to go that extra mile. I liked that about him – he kind of reminded me of Hermione Granger. I told him that once and he screeched with laughter, nodding his head. "I totally see it!"

He was good friends with a lot of my friends (he'd also been there to witness my falling-into-cow-poo incident in PE all those years ago), so when I saw that we'd been put in the same English class for Year 11, I was relieved. The class was loud and intimidating, so I was happy to have someone I knew by my side. While I was quiet, Nathan was outspoken – perhaps our teacher thought we'd balance each other out. We made a good pair, sitting right at the back of the classroom; poking fun at each other and gossiping.

One evening, I was in my bedroom watching TV when Nathan texted me out of the blue, asking about our English homework. I thought it was odd – I'd seen him write the homework details down in his planner – but I explained it to him anyway. A few minutes later, he replied.

Thanks. How are you, anyway?

I paused. Small talk was unusual, coming from Nathan.

I'm good. How are you?

I'm OK, I think, he shot back. *But can I ask you a question?*

Sure.

What was he about to ask me that was so

important? It seemed pretty serious, whatever it was. My phone beeped suddenly, making me jump. I looked down at the screen.

What do you find attractive about guys?

I frowned. I'd never talked about boys with Nathan – that was one of the reasons I got along so well with him. I thought about just ignoring the text, but I felt bad, so I just reeled off a spiel of stereotypical qualities that I thought sounded appealing – tall, dark, handsome, intelligent – the kind of guys my friends talked about. I pressed send, sighing. I felt unsettled – lying to my friends was getting more and more uncomfortable.

Ten minutes passed. Then twenty. I glanced at the clock, confused. Nathan usually replied within minutes. I read back over what I'd written. Had I said something offensive? I stared at my phone keyboard, chewing my lip.

How about you? I wrote, tentatively. *What do you find attractive about women?*

Another half an hour passed before my phone beeped again. I looked down at the screen, and my heart stopped.

Luce, I think I'm gay.

Everything around me seemed to slow down. I stared at my phone, lost for words. Nathan was ... gay? Now he mentioned it ... it all made sense. Nathan *never* talked about girls. But ... wow. I was almost embarrassed that I hadn't ever considered it. A sense of strange relief washed over me. It felt amazing, knowing that he'd trusted me enough to confess something so personal. But what would happen now? My thoughts were whirling around my head at a hundred miles an hour. If he was gay, had he noticed that I might be, too? Should I tell him how much I was struggling? How confused and isolated I felt?

No. Not now. I wasn't ready, I told myself. Not yet. I took a deep breath, trying to calm myself down. With shaking hands, I wrote out a short reply.

Wow, how long have you known? That's really awesome, Nate! I love you no matter what, OK? I'm so proud of you.

I sat on the edge of my bed, heart pounding. I couldn't keep still; my hands and feet were twitching and I felt restless, energetic even, like I was ready to run a marathon.

My phone beeped again.

Thanks, Luce, I knew I could count on you with this. I'm so lucky to have you as a friend.

I swallowed, put the phone on the table beside me and stretched out on my bed. I stared at the patterns on the ceiling, trying to relax, but my mind was reeling. What did this mean for me? I wondered whether he wanted to tell our friends. I secretly hoped he would. If he did, I'd be able to see their reaction, and then maybe I could consider telling them about how much I was struggling, too? That is, if they took it well enough. . .

I picked up my phone. Did I really want to declare anything at this point? All of a sudden, it felt very, very real. I put my phone back down. What the hell was I thinking? This was Nathan's time to shine, not mine. I wasn't ready for this. I didn't even know what *this* was yet.

Except that you're definitely not straight . . . the voice in my head shouted.

A Reaction

24

When I saw Nathan at the school gates the next morning, he looked paler than usual. He was fiddling nervously with the strap on his bag as I approached.

"Hi, Nathan!"

"Hey! Listen, I think I'm gonna tell everybody today."

I nodded, trying to hide my surprise. Already? That was quick.

As we walked to English together, we talked it over. He told me he'd known for ages, but that he'd been in denial for years. He'd thought he was bisexual at first, but realized pretty early on that he had no feelings for girls whatsoever. I listened intently. Every word hit me like a ton of bricks. He was describing exactly the way I had felt.

As we got to our English classroom, I pushed all of my thoughts away and tried to focus on the lesson. We were studying *Of Mice and Men*, taking turns to read aloud from the book, analysing the themes – but all I could do was sit there and analyse myself. I felt so stupid sitting next to Nathan, too scared to say anything, too nervous to speak up. I envied his bravery, and his ability to be himself in the face of fear. I wanted desperately to have that same courage. I wondered whether I'd ever be able to do what he was about to do.

Finally, during break, Nathan told the rest of our friends. I could see the relief on his face as soon as he'd uttered the words. His hands were shaking, but his voice was steady.

"With all due respect, Nate, I've known you were gay since I met you," Emily laughed, shaking her head with a smile.

Bel was laughing, too. "We love you no matter

what – but I'm sure you know that already!"

Nathan was grinning from ear to ear. As the bell rang and we all went our separate ways, I realized that my friends hadn't cared in the slightest. What did that mean for me? Surely they'd react the same way?

As Becci and I were walking to the school bus that afternoon after our PE lesson, I spotted Nathan coming out of the double doors behind us. I waved at him and he hurried over to us.

As he got closer, I could see he was trying not to cry.

"I hate them," he whispered, his bottom lip wobbling.

Becci and I pulled him away from the crowd, confused. "What's wrong?" Becci asked worriedly.

"The boys in my PE class," he spluttered. "Th-th-they were even worse than usual. They spent the whole lesson calling me homophobic names. And Greg Spaulding started following me around, shouting stuff, throwing things at me . . . I – I just can't believe how horrible they are. That lot think they can lord it over us, and it's only because they're so *popular* that they think they can get away with it. It never stops with them. . ."

He trailed off, blinking back tears. Greg Spaulding, amongst many others in the "popular" gang, was always making jibes at Nathan. Usually he just ignored them – their insults were pathetic, after all – but it was clear Greg had overstepped the mark this time.

"How DARE they?" Becci shouted, making people around us stop and stare. "I can't believe they think they can get away with that."

Nathan nodded. "God, sometimes I just can't wait to get out of here."

I hugged him. "Nathan, I absolutely promise you that in five years' time, you'll be in a high-flying job having the time of your life, and they'll have disappeared into nothingness. They'll probably still be living in this stupid town, going nowhere, and they'll look at you and realize how wrong they were. I promise."

Seeing my friends react the way they did had reassured me that they would love me no matter what I told them. We would protect Nathan and I knew that eventually, they would protect me, too. All I had to work on now was figuring out who I was . . . and how to be OK with that.

PROM

25

Exams were finally over, and now all we could do was wait for the results and hope for the best. I tried my hardest not to think about what grades I would get – after all, worrying wasn't going to help. Until then, I was determined to relax.

Year 11 was coming to an end, which meant only one thing: the esteemed Year 11 Prom. My friends and I had planned to go together as a big group, but out of the blue, Emily's friend Josh Barrington asked her if she would go with him, and then Bel was asked by Dean Hillier.

To my surprise, Luke Curtis asked me to go with him.

From the very beginning, there was a misunderstanding between us. I'd never really spoken to Luke before, so I assumed he wanted to go just as friends. He seemed nice enough – he was always smiling, and he was a very hard worker (I'd heard rumours that he never got lower than A grades in his exams). I accepted his offer, not thinking much of it.

"He probably has a crush on you, fool!" said Emily when I told her. "So are you gonna go with him?"

"Oh god, really? I already said yes, Em!"

"Well do you like him?!"

"As a friend, yeah. He seems cool. But no further than that!"

Emily laughed. "It'll be fine, I'm sure."

And so, just like that, I found myself going to Prom with a boy. I tried hard not to worry, convincing myself that Emily had been joking about the crush. Luke and I barely knew each other. I pushed it to the back of my mind.

On the evening of Prom, my friends came over to my house and we all got ready together. We primped and preened in front of my bedroom mirror, doing our hair and make-up, perfecting our lipstick, sticking on precarious fake eyelashes and pouting, snapping photos. Getting all glammed up was so exciting. We practised our catwalks in my cramped living room, tottering around in our high heels, sipping on glasses of champagne which my mum had prepared for us ("You get one glass each, I don't want to get into trouble!").

Clare's mum drove us there, and as we all bundled out of the car at the school gates, we could see a crowd of people in the distance. Everyone looked so glamorous in their ballgowns and three-piece suits. We walked through the crowd and a bunch of different people I'd never really spoken to before complimented me on my dress and shoes, smiling and waving like I was an old friend. All of our teachers were there, too – some of them looking unrecognizable out of their work attire. They clapped and cheered us on as we walked down the red carpet. It felt like we were attending some kind of premiere.

Once inside, I spotted Melissa in the corner with her friends. She was dressed in a floor-length purple gown, with big, fluttery eyelashes and bright red lipstick. Her hair was pinned elegantly back out of her face. She looked beautiful. She grinned at me and waved. I waved back, dazed. My feelings for her had faded completely, but there was no denying how captivating she was.

"Lucy! Hey, Lucy!" A distant voice dragged me out of my daydream. I turned around, feeling disorientated.

Luke was walking towards me, clutching a rose. His cheeks flushed as he handed it to me. All of a sudden, guilt crashed over me like a tidal wave. Up until that moment, I'd forgotten all about him.

I smiled awkwardly, not knowing what to do. "Thank you so much! Wow. It's so beautiful!"

Luke grinned. "Look, I matched my tie to your dress!"

In a desperate bid to rid myself of my guilt, I

grabbed my friends, and Luke, and headed to the dance floor. We horsed around like idiots, jiving with each other, acting like kids. Every now and then I glanced over at Luke, who was doing the Macarena with Emily's date, Josh. They were laughing uproariously. My conscience was eased just a little. As the night wore on, Luke drifted away to dance with other people. He hadn't tried to dance with me once. I desperately hoped he wasn't upset, and that he'd somehow got the message I wasn't interested. I kept accidentally catching Melissa's eye and looking away, embarrassed, hoping she hadn't seen me blushing.

At the end of the night, our little group – Emily, Bel, Kat, Clare, Becci, and I – went back to Clare's house for a sleepover. We were buzzing. We'd danced our socks off and laughed so loudly that most of us had lost our voices.

As we got in the front door, Clare's mum presented us with doughnuts, cupcakes and mugs of hot chocolate. We all squealed, rushing into the kitchen, clutching our high heels in our hands.

We sat at Clare's dining table, munching our snacks, gossiping about the evening.

"So Emily, do you think you're into Josh?" Kat asked.

"Nah. Josh's great and all, but I just see him as a friend," Emily said, sipping on her cocoa.

"It's the same with Luke," I said quickly. "I felt bad all evening – I mean, he brought me a rose, you guys! But I just don't see him in that way."

"Awww!" everyone said in unison, giggling.

"I think you'd break his little heart if you told him that!" Kat said, offering me the last cupcake.

"I just . . . I don't think I want a boyfriend right now, you know?" I laughed, nervously.

There was a pause.

"Oh no, I'm exactly the same, don't worry," said Clare. I wanted to hug her.

"Me too," Becci chimed in. "I don't want one until I've finished university . . . boys are too much work!"

We all laughed.

Clare bit her lip thoughtfully. "You know, I think I'd like to start a career before I focus on getting a boyfriend, to be honest. Priorities and all that!"

"Yeah, boyfriends come second!" Bel chortled. "Well, boyfriend, lover, whatever you wanna call them."

My heart stopped. I knew this was my chance. I made a split-second decision.

"Agreed," I said, trying to keep my voice steady. "Who cares what gender, anyway?"

I was stunned by what had just come out of my mouth. I sat stock still, holding my breath.

Nobody batted an eyelid.

"As long as they cook me dinner every night, I don't care who it is!" Bel joked, reaching for another doughnut. Everyone laughed again.

A wave of relief washed over me like a warm bath. In an instant, my exhaustion evaporated, and I stood up, suddenly restless, raring to go. I pulled on my fluffy socks and started shimmying across the kitchen floor like Michael Jackson. Clare, who was laughing so hard she had to hold on to the countertop to stay upright, joined me. We pranced around the kitchen, twirling like ballerinas, and soon enough, everyone joined in, sashaying across the floor in our pyjamas and slippers. I was elated. They didn't care! I mean, of course they didn't – no one had been bothered when Nathan came out – but something about that moment felt so life-affirming. It felt real, it felt concrete, and it felt good.

As we snuggled down in the living room that night under duvets, blankets and sleeping bags, I fell asleep feeling happier than I had done in ages. What an incredible evening it had been. A weight, however small, had been lifted off of my shoulders. Year 11 was ending on a high.

A few weeks later, when our exam results were finally posted, I was relieved to see that, despite my endless worrying and sleepless nights, I had secured myself a place in Sixth Form.

I was about to begin a new chapter of my life. It scared me a little that in just two short years, I might be attending university, but I knew I could do anything if I set my mind to it. I felt more prepared than ever for my next step.

CHELY WRIGHT

26

A whole year had passed. The end of Year 12 was imminent, and our workload had increased tenfold. A-levels were fast-approaching, and we were swamped with revision. I could feel my inner Hermione kicking in. I loved how, even several years after finishing the Harry Potter books, an imaginary character was still propelling me to work my hardest. I felt like she was my secret weapon.

Every second that we didn't spend studying, we felt guilty. Our walks home from the school bus each evening were our only moments of true freedom. We'd walk as slowly as possible, staring up at the clear blue sky, drinking it all in while we could. As soon as we got home, we had to get back to work.

As Emily and I were ambling home one evening, we decided to take a detour through the fields. We sprinted through the tall grass, sweatshirts tied loosely around our waists, school bags swinging. Flies circled lazily over the glistening tarmac, and the smell of freshly cut grass wafted past us on the warm breeze. We could see our little village in the distance, a hazy mirage of blistering heat. An ice-cream van pootled past us, its cheery little melody piercing the sluggish air. We watched it lurch around the corner, weaving its way through the narrow country roads.

We struggled on up the hill, sweaty from the heat, until eventually, we reached the Church Green. From here, you could see Emily's house – and to the left, down a side street, was mine.

"God, I hate exams," Emily sighed, defeated. "It's so typical that we have to be stuck indoors. We're nearly eighteen for goodness' sake. We should be out partying!"

I laughed. "Just a few more weeks, and we'll be free. We have the rest of the summer for partying!"

Emily nodded, sadly. "True, true. OK, I'm off to torture myself with eighteenth-century Russian history!"

We said our goodbyes and parted ways.

My house was the first on the left, a mismatched jumble of yellowing, crumbled bricks and a battered-looking Volvo in the driveway. A small family of nesting wood pigeons had made themselves a home in amongst the roof tiles, but today they were basking in the shade of the front lawn, cooing softly as I made my way up the path.

"Hey, Dad!" I said as I shut the door behind me. "It's so nice outside ... shame I have to do stupid revision."

Dad handed me a cup of tea with a sympathetic smile. "Why don't you take a break this evening, love? You need some time to breathe a little, or you'll go mad!"

I sighed. He was right – one evening off wouldn't hurt.

I padded up to my bedroom, exhausted. I watched TV for a little bit, then opened up my laptop. I scrolled down my Facebook newsfeed listlessly. I felt strangely restless and unsettled. Frustrated, I switched to Twitter in search of a distraction.

As the page loaded, I turned to look out of the window. The sky had faded from blue into a deep, intense shade of crimson, and the air had cooled a little. Fluffy indigo clouds stretched upwards and outwards endlessly, casting a fierce shadow against the ghostly half-moon. Dusk was creeping in, so I opened my window a little wider, welcoming the breeze against my skin. For a short while, I simply sat there, watching the dappled evening sunlight sparkle and dance across the rooftops.

I looked back at my computer screen, blinking as my eyes adjusted to the light.

A tweet caught my eye.

"Chely Wright, the first openly gay country singer, is here today. Her story is truly unbelievable, and very touching."

I frowned. The words "openly gay" made my palms sweaty. My heart began to beat a little faster. Should I click on the link? A familiar, nervous sensation ran up my spine. I sat back in my chair, eyes watering.

I needed to watch the video. I needed to see what this Chely Wright lady had to say. So what was stopping me? What was I scared of?

I swallowed, then nervously checked behind me before clicking on the link, plugging my headphones in hastily, turning the volume down to the quietest it would go. I waited with bated breath as the interview loaded, scrolling through the comments section.

"What a brave, inspiring young woman," one person had written. *"I hope this is a comfort to anyone watching."*

I felt a lump rise in my throat as I clicked play.

It was a clip from *The Ellen DeGeneres Show.* I'd heard of Ellen DeGeneres from some of Emily's gossip magazines, but I didn't know much about her. Chely Wright appeared to be a special guest of some sort. She looked incredibly nervous as she sat down opposite Ellen.

"*Hey, Chely, welcome to the show!*" Ellen said, grinning. I paused the video and looked over my shoulder, double checking that no one had come into the room. I pressed play.

"*Chely, I'm one of those people who can completely understand how you've felt in the past and how you must feel right now, but I'm really proud of you. That was a really brave thing to do.*"

The audience erupted into applause.

"*Thank you very much, Ellen,*" said Chely. "*I must say, I'm freaking out right now that I'm on the show – I'm a big fan of yours and you've inspired me in so many ways.*"

I couldn't take my eyes off the screen.

"*You know . . . I had recommitted myself, time and time again, to never telling anyone in my family or any of my fans that I was gay.*"

She paused.

"*That I am gay.*"

The audience erupted again.

She went on to describe her coming out process – how she had wanted desperately to tell her own father, and how, eventually, she did.

"The day I told him that I was gay, I was playing a show that evening. And later that night, he came up on stage, addressed the crowd, and said, 'I'm so glad you guys came out to see my daughter – I'm really, really proud of her.'"

I stared at the screen, mouth open, eyes wide. I was overwhelmed by Chely's honesty and compassion. She was speaking, I felt, directly to me.

"I searched my entire town for anybody who was like me – and I couldn't find anyone," Chely explained. *"But I know that right now, there is a girl sitting in her bedroom in some little town somewhere, and she's feeling like an alien."*

I blinked frantically as tears began to fill my eyes.

"I felt that it was wrong of me, really, to let people assume for one more minute that I am not gay."

The audience burst into applause once again,

shouting and whooping. I was sobbing by now, but I found myself smiling through my tears. I wanted to clap, too. I wanted more than just to clap. I wanted to shout and cheer and scream at the top of my lungs, and jump up and down in celebration of this woman who had been so compellingly well-received and understood.

"At the end of the day," said Ellen tentatively, looking directly at Chely, *"the thing that everyone asks for is to just be loved unconditionally."*

Tears were streaming down my cheeks. The interview finished, but my mind was reeling from what I'd just seen. I could hear nothing but my own ragged breath. The sound of my heartbeat was ringing in my ears and my head was pounding.

I had been grappling with this, inwardly, for seventeen years. Every second of every day I had been fighting, with all my might, against the thoughts in my head that would question, repeatedly, the validity of my sexuality, what I might be, what I could be – and it was slowly destroying me. I had used the future as a form of escape from the present, telling myself over and over that one day, things would change.

And that day, finally, was today. My eyes watered. I took a deep breath.

"I'm gay," I whispered into the dusk.

Silence. I held my breath, expecting my thoughts to come crashing down on me like an army, ready to stamp out the words the split second they had left my mouth. I waited for something to happen, some twisted, soul-destroying, earth-shattering chain reaction.

Instead, there was nothing. My thoughts were clear and my pulse was steady. I sat completely still as an overwhelming sense of tranquillity and peace washed over me like a tide.

My brain remained quiet. And for the first time in my life, I didn't fight the silence – I accepted it. Slowly but surely, the weight of seventeen years' worth of shame and toxic self-loathing floated away on the warm evening breeze.

All at once, I could breathe again.

KAELYN

27

I was on cloud nine. The sun seemed brighter, the sky looked bluer, and the air felt warmer. Exams were over, and a long hot summer of freedom stretched out in front of me. My friends and I hung out every day, sitting in Ben's back garden drinking cider, strolling down the country lanes, playing cards in our local pub without a care in the world.

One evening, having spent the day lounging around in the sun eating ice cream with my friends, I headed home in high spirits, a little sunburnt but decidedly happy. I collapsed into bed and tried my best to sleep, tossing and turning for hours before finally getting up, exasperated. It was too hot. I pulled back the curtains and opened both windows, peering up into the night sky.

I turned and reached for my phone. I opened up Tumblr and began to scroll through it, feeling dazed. Another gust of wind crept in through the window, brushing against my face, making my eyes water. It woke me up a bit. I blinked instinctively, and realized I was still standing by my window, phone in hand.

I crawled back into bed and continued scrolling until a post suddenly caught my eye. It was from a girl named Kaelyn, whose blog I'd been following for a while.

"I'm thinking of coming out to my parents soon. A few of my friends know. I'm 22 and getting ready to leave the country for the next four years for veterinary school. I think I should come out to them before I leave. But I'm terrified."

I was stunned. I'd loved her blog for ages, but I'd

had no idea she was gay. I'd never seen her mention it before. As my tiredness ebbed away and I re-read her post, I found myself smiling. Wow. This girl had been going through the exact same thing as me and I hadn't even known it. I stared at the screen, mulling it all over. It was such a comfort to know that no matter how isolated I was, or how alone I felt, I was never, truly going to be by myself. Sure, she was halfway across the world on a different continent, but here we were, going about our daily lives, experiencing the exact same feelings, thoughts and worries.

I frowned, staring at the screen, wondering if I should say something. She'd listed her email address in her 'about' section. Should I message her, just to wish her luck? Maybe tell her that I was in a similar situation? It had slowly been dawning on me that now I had accepted that I was gay, I was going to have to tell someone soon. I didn't know this girl, but we were in the same boat. What was the worst that could happen?

I decided I had nothing to lose, opened

up my laptop, and began drafting out an email.

"Hello,

I'm 17 & I live in a tiny little village in the
United Kingdom.

I came across your Tumblr through a friend,
and I immediately followed you because you
post such cool things! I love all the Taylor Swift
stuff you post, she is ah-mazing.

But just now I saw that you had made a post
stating that you were ready to come out. As I
was reading it, I could almost tell that you've
been feeling what I've been feeling for the past
17 years. It was a pain that I recognized – from
so many years of hiding, crushing it, wanting it
to go away with all the strength you can muster.
Countless nights praying and wishing and
hoping against hope that perhaps, just perhaps,
this whole 'thing' is just a phase that you'll grow
out of, something that'll pass and that you'll be
able to look back on and think, 'thank God that's
over.'

But you know what? I know that won't happen. I know what I am, I am what I am. I accept it. And it's suddenly dawned on me that I'm not alone with this.

Living in such a tiny, unknown place is hard at the best of times, but when you feel so singled out and different from the others – alien, even – it feels like the whole world is against you.

But I found you – or maybe you found me? – and because of this, because of you, I'm stronger and more determined than ever.

From the bottom of my heart, thank you.

Best wishes for the future. x"

I re-read the email at least a dozen times. My eyes were starting to get heavy again. I held my breath, swallowed, then hit send.

I shut my laptop, lay down and closed my eyes. I couldn't help but wonder what this girl was doing right now. All I knew was that she lived in America – I had no idea where – but that meant there'd be a time difference. She was probably awake right now. Maybe she was even checking her email? I found myself desperately hoping she'd reply. *It would be amazing to have a friend I could talk to about all this*, I thought, as I finally drifted off to sleep.

The next morning, I awoke bright and early. I grabbed my laptop, and opened up my email.

Inbox (1).

Heart pounding, I clicked the icon.

"Hey.

That was the sweetest email I've ever read. I applaud you for knowing who you are at seventeen . . . it took me 22 years to face the facts.

I went to a Catholic school until university and my room-mates all through college were very religious. I felt like I was always sinning, like I was lesser than they were. I dated guys until I was 19 years old, trying so hard to find that one guy that I could marry. I never knew why I felt sick to my stomach all the time, or why

I had this little piece of hatred for myself.

I actually completely shut myself off from the world. I pretended that I was focusing on school and didn't have time for friends. But in reality, I didn't want to form any new relationships in fear that I would fall in love with a girl or not fall in love with a boy. I was very pro-gay rights but never associated myself directly with those beliefs. I always kept quiet, especially with the events going on here in America – gay marriage debates, 'don't ask, don't tell,' even gay people aren't allowed to give blood here because the blood is 'tainted.' I never meant to face who I was at this time. But in a funny way, I began watching The L Word. And it made me realize that being gay isn't WHO I am, it's a part of who I am.

I am so much more than gay. By staying in the closet, I was just enabling the discrimination in this country. The more people that come out, the easier it will be for the next person. I understand what you're going through and even though I haven't come out to my parents directly, it seems like an easier task than it did before. Gay isn't the only thing that defines me.

Take your time. Don't stress about the fears you have for yourself. You're so much more than just your sexuality. I'm a sister, a daughter, a dog owner, a cook, an athlete, a movie buff, and a massive Taylor Swift fan. And I'm going to be a veterinarian. Gay just happens to be part of that.

Coming out and acceptance of yourself comes in phases, the first is denial, then it's hatred for the way you are, and then it's appreciation. Recently, I realized that I feel blessed that I am gay and it will happen to you in time.

I feel like we're both at the same place in our life right now so we can be here for each other.

Thank you for your email. I hope more people in the world are like you.

Kaelyn x"

By the time I'd finished reading the email, I had tears in my eyes. She sounded exactly like me. A movie buff, a Taylor Swift fan ... she'd even watched *The L Word*. Her words were such a comfort. I felt warm and safe, knowing that she was out there somewhere. What she had written was so sweet, and so genuine.

Heart racing, I wrote out a reply.

"Hey,

Thank you. Again. I don't know how many times I can say that without sounding stupid :)

But ... I am so happy right now. I have never, ever told anyone about this – it's such a huge, huge secret. I used to tell myself that I would tell no one ... I didn't want anyone to know – at all. You are the first person I've ever told, and I've never even met you – but it feels so brilliant to have let it out. I've never even written it down! But 17 years is a long time to keep a secret, no matter how big it is. It feels so lovely to be able to tell someone something so personal and secretive and for them to understand you, and not make judgements about you. You're the same as me – trying to hide it, trying to date guys, feeling sick to the stomach but convincing yourself it's just a phase, just butterflies or nerves? I have the same fear – that I'll fall in love with a girl and not fall in love with a boy and for it all to be so real.

Often when people come out they get accused of 'lying to the world' . . . but I don't think people are lying, I think they're scared – they're in hiding. And I don't blame them . . . but it's people like you who have taken the step forward, making it that little bit easier for the rest of us. Even though my secret is still a secret to everyone around me, I can sleep tonight knowing that someone else on earth knows . . . and they don't hate me because of it. And that's so reassuring, you would not believe. . .

I am also amazed that you, too, found comfort in The L Word – that show has never, as far as I know, been broadcast in the UK, so I only came across it by chance ... but I watched all six seasons and by the end of it I had come out as a different person. Sounds cheesy I know, but I got so involved with all the characters. Crying over Dana, feeling so happy for Bette and Tina when they had Angelica, and laughing along when Shane and Alice drew all over Shane's billboard ... all that stuff ... made me realize that being gay is just a part of me. There's so much more to a person than just their sexuality.

I want to be a writer, or film maker. I adore watching old black and white movies, or quirky foreign films that no one has heard of. I sing, I cook, I play guitar. I adore Taylor Swift too (I saw her at Wembley Arena in London on her Fearless tour last year).

Even though I've never met you, I feel like I've met someone I can talk to. Thank you for taking the time to write back.

Lucy x"

I was so happy. I'd found someone exactly like me. Sure, we were miles apart – but I now had someone I could talk to. Someone I could be honest with. Someone who, finally, would understand completely.

No matter how busy she was, Kaelyn always found the time to talk to me. When I was waking up to go to school, she'd be getting ready to go to sleep. When I came home in the evenings, she'd be about to start her day. We emailed back and forth endlessly, talked on the phone, and started Skyping, too – quietly, so no one else could hear. Hearing her voice gave me butterflies in my stomach. Talking to her quickly became the highlight of my day. Just knowing that she was there whenever I needed her was so comforting. I secretly hoped she felt the same way about me.

Kaelyn was so motivated and passionate about her career. She knew exactly what she wanted and she wasn't afraid to go out and get it. Although she was just starting vet school, she already had her life planned out. Ordinarily I might have been intimidated by how driven and determined she was, but when we began to talk about our hopes and our fears for the future, I saw a softer, more sensitive side to her. I could tell she wasn't the type of person who would open up to just anyone. I felt honoured that she'd let me see her at her most vulnerable.

She told me that all she wanted in life was to be happy and successful. I told her I wanted the same thing, and she laughed. "We make a great team then!"

The butterflies in my stomach started doing flips.

FALLING IN LOVE

28

At the beginning of August, my family and I went on holiday to a small town in Suffolk. We would be staying in a little holiday cottage with no internet, so Kaelyn and I had reluctantly said our goodbyes. For the first time in months, we wouldn't be able to talk every day.

I loved spending time with my family. We went on bike rides and explored the beaches. We ate ice creams on the promenade and went swimming in the pool – but nothing could fill the slow, dull ache of missing Kaelyn. It felt awful going to bed each night without saying goodnight to her. It felt like there was a piece of me missing. She had so quickly become a huge part of my life, and no part of me wanted that to change.

One afternoon, while my parents were reading in the living room, my brother and I headed out to the pool. The holiday cottage had a huge, rusted war bunker in the back garden, which the owners had converted into a small swimming pool. We splashed around, jumping off the side and diving for things, trying to hold our breath for as long as possible. Then we lounged around on our lilos, splashing water at each other, sipping on fizzy lemonade from cocktail glasses, sticking our little fingers out, pretending to be posh. It felt good to act like a kid again.

Laurie, who was now eleven, was telling me all about his classmates. He was at the same primary school I'd gone to, but the kids in his class sounded a lot nicer than mine had been.

"Most people are pretty cool," he said, sipping from his glass. "There are a few nasty kids, but I just stay away from them."

"Good."

"I mean, they're just horrible for the sake of it. Like, there's this kid in my class, Alec, and he has two mums. And they make fun of him but the rest of us are like, why? I don't see why people still have an issue with that. It's 2010 for goodness' sake."

A huge grin spread across my face. In just one off hand comment, my brother had once again proved to me that most people didn't seem to care about sexuality any more. I was so happy that I wanted to get up and sing. Instead, I just nodded enthusiastically.

"I couldn't agree more, little bro."

My brother, at least, would be cool with it if I told him. I breathed a sigh of relief. That was one more person I didn't have to worry about.

The day we got back home to Oxford, I ran upstairs as fast as I could and turned on my computer. I had seven emails from Kaelyn, one for each day I'd been away. She'd made a different video for me every single day, talking about what she'd been up to, and what her plans were. She ended each video by saying she missed me.

The seventh and final video was short but sweet. *"Let me know when you get this video. I want to talk to you so badly. I think . . . I think I love you."*

My heart started beating at one hundred miles an hour. I opened my phone and sent her a text.

Hey. I'm home. –L

Within minutes, she replied.

Hey you. Hope you had a good holiday –K

I smiled. My phone buzzed again.

I missed you terribly. Did you see my video?

Without hesitation, I wrote out a reply.

Yeah. I think I love you too. Can we Skype?

I felt so happy I could fly. The butterflies in my stomach were doing somersaults, and it was the best feeling in the world. We chatted for an hour over Skype. We talked about everything – how much we'd missed each other when I'd been gone, how Kae had realized she loved me the minute I had left for Suffolk, and how hard it had been not to talk to each other for a week. It felt so right. I felt so comfortable. It was like I'd known her my whole life.

"So . . . are we, like, dating now?" said Kaelyn with a grin.

"I guess so! I mean, if you want to. . ." I trailed off, laughing.

"Jeez, I never thought I'd fall in love with someone I've never even met before. Like, how can that even happen?"

"I have no idea. It's so surreal."

"And it all happened so fast! I kind of like it though. We're so twenty-first century! I'm just thankful for Skype. At least I know you're a real person and not some weirdo!" We both giggled.

And so, we decided to make it official.

I had a girlfriend!

All I wanted was to be with her. I wanted to tell everyone I knew about her. I wanted to tell people in the street. I wanted to scream it from the rooftops.

But I couldn't. Nobody knew I was gay except

Kaelyn. It hurt me deeply to have to keep her a secret. She was doing the same; only her room-mate knew about us. We spurred each other on through our most difficult days. I told her that it wouldn't always have to be like this. She told me she would wait until the end of the world if it meant she could be with me.

But as the days rushed by and winter crept in, I was starting to get restless. Should I just come out with it one lunchtime at school? I had to say *something*. I couldn't keep this a secret for much longer – it was killing me. As December rolled up, I realized that I was just going to have to bite the bullet and do it.

29

So What's She Like?

It was New Year's Eve, and my friends from the village, plus Bel who had come over from the next town, were spending the night at Ben's house. Having already been to the pub and back, we were now chilling in Ben's living room, drinking cheap champagne and beer and counting down the hours before the clock struck midnight.

I felt at peace. I was surrounded by my best friends in the entire world; people I adored and would do anything for. I had an amazing, incredible family. I had a girlfriend who loved and supported me no matter what. I was wanted, I was needed, and I was really, really happy.

As it neared midnight, Emily, Bel and I were sprawled out on the kitchen floor, passing around a bottle of champagne.

"I still can't believe we're in our last year of school," mumbled Emily, sipping from the bottle.

"Me neither. I'm so not ready for the grown-up world of university!" Bel howled dramatically, banging her fists on the floor like a child. We all giggled. There was a pause.

"Do you guys want to get boyfriends at university?" Emily asked.

I saw the chance, and in my slightly drunken state, I took it.

"No, I have a girlfriend," I said without missing a beat. I was expecting to feel the familiar nervous feeling in my stomach at any second, but I didn't. I was completely and utterly at ease.

Emily tilted her head up to face me, half-smiling. "What?"

"I have a girlfriend."

They both laughed nervously.

"WHAT?!" Mossy careered around the corner

and crashed into the fridge.

Monkey, Chris, Rachel and Ben followed suit, running into the kitchen in a drunken frenzy.

"You have a GIRLFRIEND?" Mossy screeched.

They were all looking at me incredulously.

"Yeah! I met her a couple of months ago."

"HOW? WHERE?" they all shouted in unison.

"Well . . . we met on Tumblr, which I know sounds crazy, but I promise you she isn't a creep or anything! We Skype literally every day. She's amazing."

"I didn't know you were GAY though?!" screamed Monkey. "Why did you never tell us?"

I swallowed, suddenly trying to hold back tears. "I was scared, I guess."

They all lunged at me at once, pulling me into a hug, ruffling my hair and squeezing my hands.

"Lucy, I am so SO proud of you," Bel cried, drunken tears filling her eyes. "I'm so happy that you're happy. I'm just so happy for you."

My friends bombarded me with questions.

"So what's she like?"

"She's AMERICAN?!"

"Is she pretty?!"

"Oh my god. I bet she has the COOLEST accent!"

I was so surprised and pleased by how intrigued they were. They genuinely wanted to know every detail.

"We'll support you no matter what, Lucy," said Ben. "Whoever you find yourself falling in love with – what matters is that you're happy. That's the only thing that should matter for anyone, to be honest."

Mossy, who had been quiet for quite some time, suddenly turned and left the room.

I stared after him, shocked. I looked at Ben nervously. "Is he OK, or. . . ?"

"I think he's just a bit . . . surprised."

Monkey went into the next room to talk to him. I followed him, tentatively.

"You OK, Mossy?" I whispered, worried.

"Course I am, babe. Just a bit, you know. . ." he trailed off. There was a pause. "I mean . . . so . . . you're – you're definitely gay?" His bottom lip began to wobble.

"Yeah, pretty certain. Are you OK with that?"

"Definitely. I'm so proud of you, Luce. I guess I'm just bummed that now I really don't ever have a chance to be with you. I'm sorry. I know that's selfish of me."

All I could do was hug him, because I knew exactly how that felt. I'd watched as Melissa had slipped away with someone else. I knew what a horrible sinking feeling it was, watching someone you like walk away, and knowing that you can't do a thing about it.

"You know you'll always be one of my best friends, Luce," Mossy whispered.

I hugged him tighter.

Just before midnight, Bel, Emily and I went for a walk. It was freezing outside, but we strolled up the narrow country lane arm in arm, dancing and swinging our legs. There wasn't a cloud in the sky, and when we looked up, we could see every single star. I spotted the Big Dipper and whooped with drunken delight. The moon, a tiny thin crescent in the darkness, lit up the whole sky.

"I hope you still love me, guys!" I slurred, giggling.

The other two started giggling, as if I'd said something ludicrous.

"Of course we still love you, fool!" said Emily.

We carried on walking until we reached the main road, screeching at the top of our lungs.

"Guys, guys! Look! It's nearly midnight!" said Emily, pointing to her phone. It was 23:59. We stopped and stood, huddled together, staring breathlessly upwards. There was a long pause.

Then, all at once, the sky was filled with a burst of vibrant, fiery colours; vivid reds and greens, twisting and turning in mid-air, shooting up into the sky like tiny rockets. An eruption of golds and blues followed, flaring up the darkness and casting a golden glow over the village, whizzing through the atmosphere at top speed. It was beautiful, standing arm in arm with my two best friends in the freezing cold, our eyes sparkling as the sky exploded above us, our ragged breath hanging in the air as the church bells chimed in the New Year.

I'd done it.

I had started the New Year on a high. The way Emily and Bel had reacted confirmed what I had already known deep down: they would love me no matter what. Their positivity had given me the confidence boost that I had desperately needed, and around mid-January, I decided to come out to the rest of my friends – the ones who hadn't been at Ben's party.

Nathan was astounded, and pretended to be outraged that I hadn't told him sooner.

"How DARE you keep this from me?!" he screeched dramatically, pretending to flick a scarf over his shoulder, sashaying away. He came back giggling and pulled me into a hug. "Guess we're the token gays of the group now, eh?!"

Becci, Clare and Kat were surprised – and sad that I hadn't had the courage to tell them sooner.

"I wish you hadn't kept this from us! I feel so bad that you felt like you had to keep it a secret all this time. I feel like a terrible friend for not noticing," said Becci, sadly.

"Don't be silly! You're the best friend a girl could ask for. I was just ... scared, I guess," I hesitated, looking down at my shoes. The anxiety and the panic that had plagued me for years already seemed so distant now that it was all over. The feelings had been replaced with a sense of serenity and calm. I looked up at my friends' smiling, sympathetic faces. What had I even been scared of? I could feel myself tearing up. I opened my mouth, but no words came out.

"I love you guys so much," I finally spluttered, and pulled them into yet another hug.

The message was clear: if you're happy, we're happy.

I still didn't feel ready to broach the topic with

my family yet. It was my last year at school, and then I was hopefully heading to university, which meant I'd be leaving home for the first time. I told myself that I would come out to my parents as soon as I had moved out. That way, if anything went wrong, I at least wouldn't be living at home. Deep down, I knew it was going to be absolutely fine, but the anxious voice in my head was still telling me to wait.

As the weeks went by, the thought of leaving home was gradually becoming a reality, and it terrified me. How would it feel to go somewhere completely new, away from my friends and family? What would it feel like to finally be completely independent?

"You learn a lot about yourself when you move out for the first time," my mum said, knowingly. "And a lot about other people, too!"

"You'll meet all sorts of new people and see all sorts of new things," Dad agreed, nodding. "I think it'll be really good for you!"

I'd grown up running through fields with my friends in a happy little bubble: an easy-going, relaxed, countryside life. It was time for me to see the world from outside the tiny village I'd grown up in.

I had spent for ever worrying about what I wanted to study. My passions were literature and films – so which one should I pursue? I had spent my childhood with my head in a book and I couldn't remember a day that I hadn't spent writing, reading or both. But I also adored films and film-making. I obsessed over foreign language films like *Amélie*, *Låt Den Rätte Komma In*, *Être et Avoir* and *Moulin Rouge*, as well as the old black-and-white classics by the likes of Buster Keaton and Alfred Hitchcock, and fed my passion by getting myself a job with a small company which filmed and edited wedding videos and corporate events. I loved the pressure of getting exactly the right shots at exactly the right time, and the thrill of capturing the event perfectly gave me such an adrenaline rush.

I needed to find a degree where I could study both of my favourite things. I searched for weeks, and with my dad's help, narrowed it down to five courses based on practical film-making that also included writing modules. I submitted my personal statement – and then I waited.

After what felt like for ever, two universities wrote back, both offering me a place, as long as I got the exam grades I needed.

A month later, I heard back from another two, and the conditions were the same.

But I still hadn't heard back from my first choice – Plymouth College of Art. I was getting worried.

Another few weeks passed, and finally, a letter arrived in the post. I skimmed through it excitedly. I had been called to an interview. My heart stopped. How was I going to manage this?

I spent the next month preparing. I gathered together every film I'd ever made as well as some screenplays I'd written, then spent hours practising in front of the mirror, trying to look cool, confident and calm.

"You've got this," I told myself, over and over. "You can do it."

On the day of the interview, Dad and I got the train down to Plymouth. With each passing minute I could feel myself getting more and more nervous. I tried to distract myself by looking out of the window, watching as the green fields of Oxfordshire became the lush pastures of Devon. As we reached Dawlish, the train rounded a corner, and there, right before my eyes, was the ocean – a rippling blue giant, splashing against the bright red rocks, stretching out as far as the eye could see. The view took my breath away.

Finally we arrived in Plymouth and made our way to the college, a huge white building with elegant glass windows smack bang in the middle of the city centre. With my heart in my mouth, I left Dad at reception and made my way to the interview room, clutching my folder of films and screenplays. I tried to shake off the shy, eleven-year-old Lucy, and remind myself that I was now a confident eighteen-year-old who could do anything she put her mind to. I took a deep breath, and knocked on the door.

"Ah! You must be Lucy," said the man behind the desk as I sat down. He had a calm, kind face and floppy brown hair. "I'm Paul, one of the film lecturers here."

Paul looked genuinely interested in what I had to say, and as soon as we got on to the topic of our favourite films, my confidence shot through the roof. The more I spoke, the more relaxed I began to feel. My pounding heartbeat steadied. I showed him some of the videos I'd made, and he patiently watched each of them in turn. I was amazed at how attentive and genuine he seemed. He was just the kind of person I'd love to have teach me.

As I got up to leave, he shook my hand and told me that they'd love to have me on the course. "Expect an email from us over the next couple of days!"

I smiled and thanked him, trying not to skip out of the room with elation. I rushed to find my dad.

"Knew you had it in you, Miss Lucy Sutcliffe!" he said, beaming from ear to ear and hugging me.

As I stared out of the window on the train back to Oxford that evening, I thought about the advice that Mossy had given me all those months ago. "Fake it till you make it," he'd said. I didn't quite understand what he meant at the time, but I did now. I'd never thought of myself as a confident person, but I'd gone into that interview room and acted like that was exactly what I was. And even though I'd had to fake it at first and pretend like I wasn't terrified, the confidence I'd felt as I walked out of that room was 100 per cent real.

But did that make *me* a fake? Maybe the person Paul had seen that afternoon wasn't the real me? Would he still want me on the course if he knew how scared I had been deep down?

As the train crawled back through Dawlish and the sky darkened, I wondered whether I actually *was* confident. Perhaps it was just buried underneath all my constant worrying and anxiety?

The more I thought about it, the more I became certain that it had been me in that interview room all along.

LAST
DAY
31

A few days later, at school, I received the email.

"Congratulations! You have officially been offered an unconditional place on the Film Arts BA (Hons) course at Plymouth College of Art."

My jaw dropped open. An *unconditional* offer? That meant I had a place, no matter what my grades turned out to be.

My friends, who had crowded around my computer, starting whooping and clapping.

"That's amazing, Luce!" Becci said, staring at me in disbelief.

I was astounded. I felt like I was in a dream. I couldn't wait to tell my family and Kaelyn.

The summer holidays were imminent, and my final year at school was coming to an end. But despite the fact that I knew it had been coming for months, I hadn't quite prepared myself for just how emotional it was going to be when the very last day finally rolled around.

Over the last couple of months, I'd been making my friends a leavers' video. I'd taken each of them aside and asked them to film a message for the rest of the group, and then I'd edited it all together and made everyone a copy to keep as a sort of time capsule. I wanted to be able to remember all of our amazing memories for years to come.

As we gathered in the film studies office and watched the video together for the first time, none of us could believe it was actually our very last day. It was amazing to be together, listening to all of the memories and in-jokes that we'd had with each other over the years.

"Remember that time we turned up to that

Halloween Social before ANYONE else got there?" Bel said.

We all groaned, remembering our embarrassment.

"Oh my god, I'd forgotten about that!" said Emily, putting her head in her hands. "We got there before the BOUNCERS had even arrived ... so we all crouched in the backseat of Clare's mum's car and hid till other people turned up ... oh god, oh god..."

"Don't forget the time we made an entire film about a pair of killer tights," I said, grinning. "Then presented it to the class with completely straight faces..."

We fell about laughing.

Bel, Emily and I decided to head to McDonalds for lunch. "Let's order Happy Meals!" said Bel, grinning. "I'm not ready to be an adult yet!"

We went up to the counter. "Hi!" I said. "Can we have three Happy Meals please?"

The surly cashier raised an eyebrow. "Might need to elaborate on that," he snorted loudly, looking around him to see if any of his colleagues had heard his hilarious comeback.

Before I could open my mouth, Bel stepped in front of me. "OK then. We'd like three VERY Happy Meals."

The cashier stared at her, open-mouthed.

Emily and I were in stitches.

I was going to miss my friends so much.

As our final day came to an end, the whole year group gathered on the school field for an afternoon of activities. There was a hot dog stand and some of the students had put out a slip 'n' slide. People were taking turns to run down it, screaming with laughter as they collapsed in a heap at the bottom. My friends and I formed a small circle on the grass nearby and sat down, throwing our bags into the middle, stretching our legs.

Kat got up to join in with the slip 'n' slide fun.

As she reached the back of the queue, Greg Spaulding stepped forward and put his arm out to stop her. "Uh, no. This isn't for people like you."

She stared at him, open-mouthed. A few girls standing behind Greg tittered.

Kat turned on her heel and marched back towards us. "Did you hear that?" she fumed. "What did he mean, 'people like me'? God, I'm so glad we're leaving today." She put on a dramatic, whiney voice. "I don't think I can stand being around *people like him* for much longer."

"We're not popular, that's why," Bel said, glaring at Greg. "But could we really expect anything more from idiots like him?"

"Don't let them get to you on our last day, Kat," I said. "They're not worth it."

We spent the rest of the afternoon chatting, snacking on ice cream that we'd bought from the corner shop, trying to ignore the loud comments from Greg and his cohort, aimed in our direction.

Then I spotted Nathan walking towards us and waved at him to come over.

"Ew, get away, you dirty gay!" Greg Spaulding shrieked as Nathan passed by the slip 'n' slide.

Nathan didn't flinch. He stared straight ahead

and kept walking, pressing his lips together so hard that they turned white.

He reached us, and sat down without saying a word. He breathed out, slowly, staring at the ground. "Only half an hour to go and I'll never have to see these people again," he said quietly. The tone of his voice wasn't one of defeat – in fact, he sounded triumphant. It was clear he no longer cared what anyone thought or said.

I still felt terrible for him. I hadn't been "out" to the rest of our year group the way Nathan had, and the likes of Greg had made his life a misery.

"We're going to go further than any of them, you know," I said firmly, looking him in the eye.

He nodded defiantly. "Yup," he said. "Just give it a couple of years."

We looked back at Greg. He'd brought out a bucket of water and unceremoniously dumped it over Colin Berk. They both started hurling water at each other, sniggering. Dozens of people started to join in.

"WATER FIGHT!" someone screeched from

over by the slip 'n' slide, making us all jump.

"I guarantee if we tried to join, we'd get yelled at," Bel said, half-laughing at the absurdity of it all.

"Shall we just go home?" Becci asked, nervously. "Why stay somewhere we're clearly not welcome?"

"Because this is our school, too, and we have every right to be here," Bel said, angrily.

"I wonder why they're suddenly so open about their dislike for us? Sure, we've never really seen eye to eye, but this is blatant bullying," I muttered.

"It's because it's our last day. They can't get sanctioned so they're doing what they want," said Emily.

The last bell rang, and we started packing up our things. As we stood up and brushed ourselves down, we took one last look at the school building in the distance. From where we'd been sitting on the field, it already seemed so tiny and far away.

All of a sudden, I heard giggling from behind me. I turned around to see Greg and Colin sprinting towards us, a bucket of water in each hand. Within seconds, they'd dumped all four buckets over us. We were soaked. They laughed uproariously as we stood there, dripping wet, humiliated.

It felt awful to end on such a sad note. As we walked away, still drenched, I looked over my shoulder to see the school building dipping out of sight. Just as we turned the corner, Bel suddenly spoke up.

"Guys, remember what Miss Bale told the six of us this morning? She said we're going to have glittering careers. That's what we need to focus on right now – not these stupid kids from school."

I nodded.

"Just wait."

THE TRAVEL BUG

32

For several months, Becci, Clare and I had been planning a trip to America. It was the last summer that we'd have together before we all left home for university, and after weeks and weeks of intensive planning and preparation, we decided to travel across the west coast, seeing as many places and doing as many things as we could. I'd never been to the States and was bubbling with excitement.

And now, there was another reason for my excitement.

Kaelyn had started her four-year veterinary medicine course at Ross University in St Kitts, a tiny island in the Caribbean. I desperately wanted to meet her for the first time, so right at the last minute, we decide to add another six days to our trip, stopping off in St Kitts before heading back to London.

I was finally going to meet her!

We started out in San Francisco, exploring the city by hopping on and off of trams, and eating hot, salted pretzels and corn dogs by the pier. We visited Alcatraz, played tug of war on the beach with the locals on Independence Day, and walked over the Golden Gate Bridge, completely awestruck.

After a few days, we joined a group tour, which would take us across three different states in six days. The first stop on our whirlwind tour was Yosemite National Park. We hiked along the trails and stood underneath the freezing cold waterfalls, yelping as the water hit our backs. We quickly got to know the other people on the trip, and by the second day, we were chatting and joking together as if we were old friends. We got on particularly well with Leo, an Australian in his mid-twenties, who was travelling around America by himself. The four of us sat at the back of the minivan, listening to music and poking fun at each other's accents.

"Say 'water' again," Leo would laugh, staring at us in disbelief as we exaggeratedly enunciated each letter at him.

Over the next few days, we camped out by Mono Lake, then travelled down and spent a day exploring Death Valley in temperatures so scorching we could barely breathe. We headed across to Nevada and down to Las Vegas, where we somehow managed to get into the casinos despite being underage (although this may have had a lot to do with us sneaking in using the back entrance). We pretended to gamble (we had no idea what we were doing, which Leo found hilarious), relaxed by the pool and enjoyed the luxuries of a hotel after five solid days of camping.

I was having an amazing time, but I was missing Kaelyn so much it hurt. There was an aching gap in my heart that only she could fill. We hadn't been able to speak since I'd arrived in America; we had been camping in places so remote that the nearest wifi spot was miles away. To ease the pain of missing her, I kept telling myself that in just over two weeks, I'd be able to see her – see her in real life – for the first time. With every passing day, I got more and more excited. I was counting down the hours, willing every second to tick by faster so I could finally hold her in my arms for the first time.

I desperately wanted our first meeting to be perfect, but the anxious part of my brain kept pointing out how much there was to be worried about. *Are you going to click in real life?* it shouted. *What if she's nothing like you'd imagined?*

I told the voice to shut up. After all, we had talked nearly every single day for over a year – why would it be any different in person? The rational side of my brain managed to keep me calm. *You'll be fine,* it kept whispering, over and over. *Absolutely fine.*

On one of our last days in America, our tour group stopped off in Kingman, Arizona, and we set up camp by a small part of Lake Havasu. It was so hot that we couldn't even be bothered to put up tents, so we decided instead to just sleep under the stars. As dusk fell, we sat around the campfire toasting s'mores, sipping on cheap beers, watching the sparks dance and fly in front of us.

As the sky gradually darkened, Leo stood up, a mischievous grin on his face. He brushed himself down and stared round the circle, chortling at our dishevelled, sweat-glazed faces.

"I'm going to melt if I sit by this fire any longer. Anyone fancy a dip in the lake?"

He didn't have to ask twice. In an instant we were on our feet and sprinting over to the embankment, falling over ourselves to get into the lake as fast as possible. Still fully clothed, we splashed and shrieked as the cool water washed over us, calming our sunburnt skin, easing our tired minds.

We lay floating on our backs, staring up at the starry sky in silence. For a few short minutes, I stopped counting down the seconds until I would be with Kaelyn, and was able to just live in the moment.

"How has it taken us this long to start travelling? We need to do this every other month!" I said out loud, to no one in particular.

"I know! I'd love to see more of the world," said Clare thoughtfully, making tiny waves with her hands, swishing them back and forth.

"Hey, you three! CATCH!" Leo shouted, interrupting our thoughts. He was standing way out in the distance, almost up to his neck in water. He threw a beer bottle in our direction and Clare caught it expertly, laughing, and cracked it open on a rock.

"I've well and truly caught the travel bug," said Becci, sipping on the beer as we passed it round. "I just want to see everything!"

I smiled. I was amazed at how much just six short days of travelling, exploring parts of the world I'd never seen before, had changed me. It had given me bounds of energy and confidence, giving me a glimpse of things as a whole for the first time. I could suddenly see the bigger picture. Suddenly, I felt ready to take on whatever was about to be thrown at me.

Everything I had done in my life so far – every thought, dream, idea and action – had brought me to that very spot, on a sweltering July evening, paddling in a lake, star-gazing with some of my very best friends alongside a group of people I barely knew. For six days and six nights, the eleven of us had been to the same places and seen the same things – but we'd each lived it in a slightly different way. And it was at this point – as I lay floating on my back in Lake Havasu – that I realized how much our life stories are constantly criss-crossing. I'd spent years stuck in a spiral of perpetual, toxic hatred for myself and my sexuality, but not once had I stopped to think about how many millions of other stories were being played out in parallel alongside mine. Perhaps it was the full moon, the beer I'd just drunk, or the gentle sound of the waves lapping against the shore – but something about that night made my realisation feel that little bit more profound.

Although there is no way I will ever meet every person whose story has crisscrossed with mine, I know for a fact that because our stories have touched – even just for a millisecond – I will never be completely alone.

WHAT
TOOK
YOU
SO
LONG?

33 ♥

The morning of July 16th felt like any other morning. Our group tour was over, and having said our teary goodbyes to all the lovely people we'd been travelling with, we spent a couple of days exploring Los Angeles just the three of us again, exploring the shops and beaches, hiking up to the Hollywood sign, and prancing down the Walk of Fame, batting our eyelashes, pretending to be famous.

At the end of the day, we sat perched on our suitcases outside our hostel, waiting for our taxi to arrive. The air was a little colder than usual, but the sun shone brightly, and we munched on sandwiches and hot coffee from Starbucks.

"Are you nervous to meet Kaelyn for the first time?" Becci asked excitedly, taking a swig from her cup.

I thought for a minute. "Weirdly, no! Not just yet, anyway. I thought I would be, but to be honest, I'm just really excited to finally see her."

"Awwww!" they both cooed. "That's so cute!"

Our taxi finally arrived and we piled into it, heading for LAX. We were flying from Los Angeles to Miami, then catching a plane from there to St Kitts. I kept waiting for my nerves to kick in, but they didn't. I took it as a sign, and told myself to stop worrying. After all, I had no reason to. Every minute was a minute closer to seeing Kaelyn.

We arrived in Miami airport several hours later, exhausted from the flight, but in high spirits. As we checked in, dropped off our luggage and went to find our gate, I could hardly contain my excitement. We sat in a row by the departure gate and people-watched to pass the time, making up little stories about passers-by, trying not to laugh as our anecdotes got more and more ridiculous.

Outside, a storm was brewing.

We watched through the airport lounge windows as the sky grew steadily darker. It began to rain heavily, lashing at the glass, making it rattle. I shivered. Our boarding time came and went, and another half an hour passed. Finally, the desk clerk cleared her throat and pressed the intercom button nervously.

"Ladies and gentlemen, I'm sorry to announce that American Airlines flight 318 is going to be delayed by several hours. The plane is experiencing some mechanical issues that our maintenance team are currently working on. We'll do our best to keep you updated. Thank you for your patience."

All at once, my stomach started doing backflips. Delayed? How much longer was this going to take? I didn't know how much longer I could bear it. Kaelyn and I had spent thirteen long months apart, and several extra hours shouldn't have made much of a difference, but it did. Every minute that went by felt like a whole extra day. I told myself to remain calm, but my nerves were starting to get the better of me. I tried to connect to the internet so I could text Kaelyn, but the message wouldn't send. After several attempts, I stopped trying. All I could do was hope that she was tracking the flight status online.

American Airlines had given every passenger a voucher for free slices of pizza as an apology. Becci, Clare and I scoffed our pizzas down, keeping busy by reading or looking out of the window, trying not to think about how long we had left to wait. The anticipation was getting to me. I could feel myself starting to panic. My stomach was churning and I felt like I was going to be sick.

Six hours and countless slices of pizza later, the desk clerk announced that they were ready to start boarding. I breathed a long, heavy sigh of relief. I had thought the moment was never going to come.

We finally took our seats – we'd been lucky enough to get a row of three. Clare squeezed my hand, and Becci smiled at me sympathetically. I was so grateful that they were by my side to help calm me down and keep me sane.

The plane's engine kicked in and the pilot asked us to fasten our seatbelts. I peered out of the window, breathing in through my nose and out through my mouth slowly, trying to relax. It was finally happening.

The pilot steered the plane out on to the runway. It was completely dark by now, and all I could see beyond the rain-soaked window were the bright yellow lights on the tarmac below us, whizzing by as the plane gained speed. Within seconds, we were up in the air, and as I looked out, everything already seemed minuscule.

The plane journey was only four hours long, but by the time we landed, I felt like I'd been stuck up there for a lifetime. St Kitts airport was tiny – one room for security, one room for luggage, and one large waiting area with a couple of vending machines. There seemed to be one lone official running everything, so going through customs took another two hours. My nerves were at breaking point, but as we finally got through security and the three of us collected our luggage, I got a sudden surge of confidence. In a few seconds, I would be with her.

We turned right out of the double doors, and there she was, standing smiling at me, her eyes sparkling.

I ran into her arms.

"Hey sweetheart," she whispered in my ear. "What took you so long?"

I felt tears of happiness swelling in my eyes, but I bit my lip and held them back, smiling at her, trying to take it all in. I couldn't believe it. Here she was, standing right in front of me, for the first time ever. I could tell she was thinking the exact same thing. I wanted to sing, and scream, and jump up in the air with excitement all at once.

Kaelyn had brought her friend Belinda with her, who gave us each a huge hug.

"Kaelyn's told me so much about y'all," she gushed. "It's so awesome to meet some real-life

Brits!"

We were all starving, so we bought chicken nuggets from a local takeaway, then bundled into Belinda's car. Kaelyn's apartment was extremely small, so Clare and Becci were going to sleep at Belinda's house across the road. We parted ways, with plans to meet the next morning for breakfast and a day on the beach.

I couldn't believe it. This was real. This was happening.

Being with Kaelyn in real life was exactly how I had imagined it would be: easy. I had been worried it might be uncomfortable or awkward, but we just picked up from where we had left off on Skype without batting an eyelid. We spent the rest of the evening watching movies, eating chicken nuggets, and cuddling with Alfie, a black kitten she'd adopted soon after moving to St Kitts.

I felt like I'd known her my whole life.

The next six days were like a dream. St Kitts was stunningly beautiful – the entire island was made up of rich, dark rainforests and long, white beaches dappled with sunlight. The sea was warm and the air was hot, and it felt like we'd stepped into paradise. Together with Becci and Clare, we hiked through the mountains, sunbathed by the water, sipped on cocktails, ate lobster fresh from the sea, and stuffed our faces with sushi each night. I'd brought my video camera along with me (I'd been filming little clips every day since we first arrived in America), and Kaelyn and I decided to film all our adventures, so we'd have something to look back on when we were apart again.

We spent every waking moment together, and every single day I fell more and more in love with her. I loved her laugh, the way her big brown eyes crinkled up when she smiled, and the way she tucked her hair behind her ear absent-mindedly whenever she was thinking. She was quick-witted and extremely smart, yet hilariously clumsy and silly. One night, she decided she wanted to cut her hair, and started hacking at it with a pair of kitchen scissors, slicing off huge chunks and then haphazardly trimming all the mismatched strands to the same length.

"Whaddya think?" she asked, giving me an extravagant curtesy.

I loved the way she snuggled up to me at night when we were sleeping, and how peaceful she made me feel. Our first kiss was better than I could have ever imagined. She rested her head on my shoulder as the cold night air brushed against our flushed faces. We stood there for ages, just breathing in how it felt to be so close to one another. I felt giddy with happiness, wishing that the feeling could last for ever.

With each day that passed, we could see the end of our trip looming closer and closer. We'd had the time of our lives, and saying goodbye meant the little piece of paradise we'd built for ourselves was about to come crashing down. Time flashed by; minutes ticked past like seconds, hours slipped through the cracks without us even noticing, and Tuesday, our last day together, swiftly rolled around. It was time to say goodbye.

I started packing up my things, trying to hold back my tears, but I didn't get very far. We spent most of the morning crying, cuddled up in bed, holding on to each other for dear life.

"I don't want you to leave," she kept whispering. "Please don't leave."

I held on to her tighter.

Eventually, I dragged myself out of bed and managed to cram everything into my suitcase. I stood in the middle of Kaelyn's room, looking around. It already felt emptier without all my stuff strewn about. I spotted her hoodie, slung over the back of a chair. I went over and held it close to me, breathing in her smell, trying to commit it to memory. Kaelyn gently took it from me, turned to her dressing table, and spritzed the hoodie with her favourite perfume.

"Here," she said, handing it back to me. "Take this with you. It'll remind you of me, even when we're thousands of miles apart."

I unzipped my suitcase, pulled out my sweater,

and did the same thing with my perfume. She held it to her chest, eyes brimming with fresh tears. We stood there, hands clasped, foreheads pressed together. Every part of me was aching with the thought of having to leave her.

"It's time to go," she whispered.

When it finally came for us to part ways at the airport, I held on to her for as long as I could. Walking away from her, as she stood there, crying, was one of the most painful experiences of my life. I felt like I was leaving half of me behind.

"We have to keep going," I whispered, holding back my own tears. "We'll be together again soon. And whether those seconds fly by like the wind, or drift on for what seems like for ever, you will always, always be on my mind, and in my heart. And that's something this stupid distance will never ever break."

"We'll be together again soon, my love," she said. "So soon."

As I boarded the plane, Clare and Becci at my

side, I looked out and spotted her, still standing by the exit. She was clutching my jumper. I waved, biting my lip, trying not to cry again.

The cabin crew shut all the exits, and we sat back and prepared for take-off.

"You OK?" Clare whispered as the plane turned on to the runway. I nodded.

Within minutes, we were up in the air. I stared out of the window at the island below, watching it shrink to the size of a pinprick before finally disappearing as the plane soared above the clouds. My heart felt like it was breaking in two. Everything had stopped the moment that our lips had parted and our hands had unlinked. Life seemed to slow down. I was being forced back into the real world.

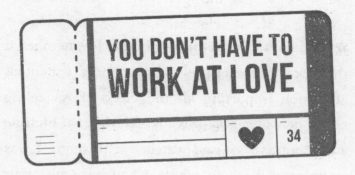

YOU DON'T HAVE TO WORK AT LOVE

♥ 34

As time passed, I began to realize something. Sure, being away from the person I loved was one of the worst feelings in the world – but I was still *lucky*. I'd found someone amazing. I'd found someone I could trust and rely on, who adored me and would keep me safe. One of the last things Kaelyn had said to me was, "You have to work hard at a relationship, but you don't have to work at love. When you think about it like that, we have it easy!"

It was true. The reality of long distance was hard, but we were desperate and willing to make it work. We were a part of something new, something magical, and I had never been more excited.

Several days after returning home, I remembered the footage I'd captured on my camera. I spent an afternoon importing all the video clips, feeling nostalgic. The trip already felt like a lifetime away, but as I sat and watched it through, I was transported back to where I had been just four weeks ago – exploring California, sitting under the stars in Arizona, walking along the Vegas Strip in Nevada, and finally, exploring St Kitts with Kaelyn.

I decided I wanted to turn my footage into a little film. It was great practice for my degree, which I would be starting in just a matter of weeks. I began piecing the clips together, bit by bit, colour correcting certain shots and adding music and title cards here and there. Halfway through, I suddenly had an idea. Why not keep the America shots and the St Kitts shots separate? I could put together a different video, of just the things I'd captured in St Kitts, and surprise Kaelyn with it. We were both struggling with how much we missed each other, and I knew this would be the perfect way to cheer her up.

I spent all evening editing. I kept the film short and sweet, with a few clips from our favourite days on the beach, and then some shots of us goofing around, imitating each other's accents. I added two of our favourite songs as the backing tracks – "Ours" by Taylor Swift, and "For the First Time" by The Script. Watching it back made me cry – it was perfect. I uploaded it on to YouTube, setting it as private so only Kaelyn could view it, then opened up a new email.

"Surprise," I wrote. *"Here's a little something to remind us of the good times. I love you."*

I hit send. I was so excited for her to see it. I knew she had been in class all day, and with the time difference, I'd be asleep by the time she got home, so I went to bed, excited to wake up to her reaction the next morning.

At around 2 a.m., my phone bleeped and woke me up. Kaelyn had sent me an email. I opened it, still half asleep.

"I'm crying so hard right now. That was beautiful,

babe. *Thank you for surprising me with that. We should film all our trips together! Such a nice way of remembering it all. I love you."*

That little film had done what I'd needed it to do – cheer us up, and spur us on. It had reminded us what really mattered: we were going to be together again soon.

There were just a few short weeks of the summer holidays left before my first term at university began. Something about the fact that I was about to leave home for the first time had made me suddenly want to be eleven years old again, with no responsibilities. I was terrified to leave, but equally as excited for what was to come.

In the evenings, my friends and I gathered together, disposable barbeques in hand, and headed to the fields. We sat around in a circle and sipped on ciders, toasting sausages and burgers over the smoky flames. We ate marshmallow sandwiches like little kids, giggling as they melted in our hands and mouths, covering us in sticky goo. We lay down and looked up at the sky, cuddled up under blankets, and talked about the future. It felt weird knowing that we probably wouldn't see each other again until Christmas.

I was about to say goodbye to the "teenage" portion of my life for good. It was time to start a new chapter.

On September 9th, I moved into 35 Seymour Avenue, Plymouth. It was a terraced student house at the top of a hill, with four bedrooms, a tiny kitchen, and a little garden with a grotty outside toilet. My new housemates were called Sean, Rob and Grace. We'd exchanged a few emails, but I was still very nervous to meet them in real life for the first time.

Our first night together went better than I had expected. My parents had slipped a bottle of wine into my suitcase – "a friendship offering!" Mum had joked – so I cracked it open in the kitchen.

I was welcomed with a cheer. The awkwardness melted away as we started getting to know each other, and we spent the evening drinking wine and beer, eating pizza, and playing several furiously competitive games of Uno. I'd put myself into confident mode, and it felt almost natural. Sure, I could be shy, but there was also an outgoing side of me that loved socializing and making friends. That night, I fell asleep feeling happy and content. It felt good to be independent and self-sufficient. I had had fun with my new housemates, and I had a feeling that I was going to love Plymouth, with its charming jumble of elegant modern architecture, church ruins and ancient office buildings, with the glittering ocean as a backdrop.

Now all I had to conquer was my first day of university.

On the morning of the day my course began, I woke up extra early. I always felt far less anxious when I had plenty of time and didn't have to rush, so I'd planned my outfit the day before and laid everything out on my desk, ready to pack into my bag. As I got ready, I stared at myself in the mirror. I was trying to stay calm, but my stomach was doing backflips.

"You can do this," I whispered to my reflection. "They want you there. They gave you a place for a reason."

I shut the front door behind me and headed down the hill. It was a bright, sunny day, and there wasn't a cloud in the sky. As I approached the university building, I took several long, deep breaths. *You're here because you're good enough*, I kept thinking to myself, over and over.

The film studio where all our lessons would be was on the second floor. The door was wide open, and as I walked in I was greeted by a tall, tanned, blond boy, with a face covered in freckles. "Hi! I'm Jacob," he said, holding out his hand. "What's your name?"

"I'm Lucy," I said, smiling.

He smiled back. "Nice to meet you, Lucy!"

A girl walked in – the only other girl in the room so far, I noticed. She was small, with brown hair and glasses. I thought about going over to say hello, but my shyness suddenly got the better of me. She went and sat down at a different table, and got chatting to some other boys.

More and more people were filing into the room, including another two girls. I wondered whether they already knew each other, and suddenly I began to worry. What if everyone was already friends, and I was the odd one out? I wasn't from around here, after all. Had I made a big mistake?

Before I had time to really start panicking, Paul, our lecturer, walked in.

"Hello everybody!" he said. "Good to see you're all getting to know each other already. Take a seat, and let's get started!"

I listened intently as Paul outlined each of the modules we'd be taking and the equipment we were going to be using. Some of it I'd never even heard of. Then we started talking about what film meant to us. It was an escape, Paul said, as well as a means of expression. A chance to get creative. To think outside of the box, and to stretch yourself to your abilities. I could feel myself smiling. That was exactly what I wanted to hear.

I left class that day feeling over the moon. I'd never been so certain that I was in the right place at the right time. I was studying something I loved, in a place I already loved, and I was going to work as hard as I possibly could.

36
HONESTY

It had been nearly a month since I'd moved to Plymouth. On the way home from class one afternoon, one of my classmates, Rex, caught up with me.

"Hey! I think we live in the same direction. Wanna walk home together?"

"Sure!"

As we walked, we chatted about our favourite books and films. We had similar taste in both: he loved Harry Potter and terrible horror films, but had a soft spot for Disney. I laughed at him for that and he pretended to be offended.

Over the coming weeks, Rex and I became

inseparable. We hung out every day, getting coffee in the mornings, wandering around Plymouth, exploring new places and talking about anything that came into our heads. We were having a blast, but there was one thing that was bothering me. I'd promised myself that I would be honest with people about my sexuality, but it hadn't come up in conversation with anyone yet. I knew that if I was going to continue being friends with Rex, I'd have to tell him. It felt wrong to keep part of my life a secret.

The very next morning, Rex and I were sat in class together, talking about celebrities.

"So, what kind of famous people do you go for? Are you a Ryan Gosling kind of girl or are you more into Zac Efron types?"

I saw my chance.

"Oh! I'm actually gay. So . . . I'm more into Emma Watson, Ellen Page types, ha ha!"

"Oh."

There was a pause.

"What do you mean, oh?" I laughed nervously.

"Nothing."

I swallowed. I'd never received a reaction like this before. Rex didn't speak to me much for the rest of the lesson, and we didn't walk home together, either. I was confused, and worried. Was this the end of our friendship? I certainly didn't want to continue being friends with him if this was the way he was going to treat me.

That evening, he called me up out of the blue.

"Hey."

"Hi?"

"Listen, I don't care that you're gay," he blurted out. "It's just, my mum is gay. And it made things hard for me for a while."

"Oh! That's OK," I said. I didn't want to ask him about the details. It seemed like a sensitive subject.

"But like I said . . . I don't care."

I was relieved. He didn't mind that I was gay. That was what mattered, right?

I very quickly got used to being upfront about my sexuality. When we'd go out to clubs or bars and guys would come up to me and ask for my number, I'd be honest about it straight away and then, with a huge smile on my face, I'd tell them about Kaelyn.

Not everyone took the hint though. One evening I was sitting at the bar with my housemates, Sean, Rob and Grace, when a spray-tanned, leather-clad man came sauntering up behind us and tapped me on the shoulder.

"Hey pretty lady," he growled, staring at me

from underneath his eyebrows.

"Um . . . hello!" I said, bemused.

"You got a boyfriend then, or can I have you?"

I grimaced. Can he *have* me? Gross.

"Nope, no boyfriend. I have a girlfriend, though. . ." I trailed off, unsure of what to say next.

He stared at me, confused.

"I'm a lesbian."

He frowned.

"I like WOMEN," I said.

My housemates, who had been watching from the other end of the bar, were in stitches.

"Oh, you like *women*?" He made air quotes with his fingers.

I stared at him in disbelief, trying not to laugh. "No, like, *actual women*. No air quotations necessary. Is there a way I could make this clearer for you?"

He smirked. "Well, I like *actual women* too. We're perfect for each other." He laughed loudly at his own joke.

I smiled politely. "I don't think so."

"OK, I see, you're playing hard to get. Can I at

least have your number?"

I was getting impatient. I opened my mouth, ready to hit him with a flurry of insults, but Sean suddenly stood up.

"Did you hear her? She said she's GAY," he said. "Gay! Gay for WOMEN! Are you a woman? No!"

The man stared, sizing Sean up, then snorted loudly.

"Just leave," Sean and I said in unison.

The man turned on his heel and strutted off.

"Jeez," said Sean. "I'm embarrassed to be a part of the male species sometimes!"

I laughed.

It felt liberating, having hidden my sexuality for so long, to suddenly be so ... proud of it. And I *was* proud – very proud. It had taken a while, but my pride had crept up on me, very slowly, and the feeling had steadily swelled inside my chest until I was ready to scream it from the rooftops. Now that I was proud, I knew it was time to do the thing I had been dreading the most: come out to my parents.

Kaelyn and I had talked it through for hours and

hours. I wanted to Skype them, but I was scared that if they reacted badly, it would make things awkward. Eventually, after much deliberation, I decided to send them an email.

I've received criticism, having retold this story to people, that coming out in an email is "chickening out." I believe whole-heartedly that this is not the case – quite the opposite. The bottom line is, coming out is an incredibly personal thing. Absolutely no one should have a say in how you go about it, except you. It's a choice you have to make, and you do it when *you* feel ready and comfortable, in the way *you* deem fit. There is no wrong or right way, and it should never be rushed. Take all the time you need.

"Do it the way you feel most comfortable with, babe," Kaelyn had said to me. "This is about you, right now. Oh, and my one piece of advice? Don't tell your parents that you're gay just as you're about to board a plane."

Kaelyn had come out a short while before. She'd gone back home to Michigan for a few weeks to visit her family, and had promised herself that she would do it. But the days ticked by and with each passing minute, she grew more and more anxious. She worked herself up into a panic, and time and time again, she tried and failed to come out and say it. Eventually, as her parents were driving her back to the airport, she knew she had to just blurt it out. She checked in, dropped off her baggage, and turned to her parents just before heading through security.

"Mom, Dad. I have something to tell you."

Her parents had looked at her in horror. "Are you pregnant? Have you done something illegal? Have you dropped out of school? What on earth is wrong?"

"No, no, it's none of those things. I'm . . . I'm gay."

They hugged her, told her they loved her no matter what, and asked her why she hadn't told them sooner. Kaelyn started crying too, and explained that she had been worried they wouldn't love her any more if they knew that she was gay. She suddenly wanted to tell them everything – all the times she'd cried herself to sleep at night, all the times she'd looked in the mirror and hated what she saw in the reflection. She wished she had more time to talk it through with them, but her gate was announced and she had to go. They said goodbye tearfully, and that had been that.

Kaelyn's parents had been a little surprised, but they loved her, and they were proud of her. I hoped and prayed that my coming out would go the same way. I picked a date – October 14th – and I promised myself I would do it then.

Dear Mum and Dad...

On the evening of the 14th, I locked myself in my room and logged on to Skype. With help from Kaelyn, I began drafting my coming out email. My heart was pounding, my palms were sweaty, and I felt like I was going to be sick.

"I don't know if I can do this. I don't even know what to put. This is so hard."

"Why don't we Google it?" Kaelyn suggested, opening up a webpage on her computer. "I'm sure other people have done the exact same thing. I bet there are tons of coming out emails you could take inspiration from."

We Googled around for hours, reading other people's coming out stories, copying and pasting bits that I liked into my draft.

"What if this goes wrong?" I whispered. "What if my life is ruined?"

"Luce, your parents are amazing. This isn't going to go wrong. They adore you. If, for some ridiculous reason, this doesn't turn out the way you want it to . . . just remember that J.K. Rowling quote. How does it go? *'Rock bottom was the very foundation upon which I rebuilt my life.'* Something like that. No matter what happens, things will get better. I mean, worst comes to the worst and they have you exiled, you can come and live with me."

I sighed. She was right. I knew my parents well enough to be confident that this would not be a big deal to them. I'd hyped it up in my head, snowballing my worries until they had completely got the better of me.

Several hours later, I finally finished writing. I'd looked over my draft so many times that the lines had started to blur. "Ugh, this doesn't even make sense to me any more," I muttered. "I've read it so many times that it looks like it's written in another language."

I copied and pasted what I'd written and sent it to Kaelyn.

"It's perfect, Luce."

I took a deep breath. This was it. "I think it's time."

"Do it," Kaelyn said, looking straight at me.

I hit send.

"Dear Mum and Dad,

I am writing you this letter because I have something quite important to tell you. Just to stop you worrying, everything is quite all right. I am not bankrupt, pregnant, addicted to drugs, starving, or ill in any way.

I am truly happy. I love both of you so much and I could not have asked for better, more supportive, patient parents. But what I wanted to tell you is that I am gay.

This letter has been drafted, scrapped, re-written and re-edited beyond recognition since 2007/8. With everything that's been going on over the years there never seemed like a good time to bring it up. I wanted to wait until things settled down, and until I felt comfortable enough to share this part of my life with you.

Please understand that my reasoning for not telling you until now is entirely based around my own paranoia, my own worry and terror, as opposed to you or the way you have brought me up. I have absolutely no idea what your views are on this subject. Sending this is a giant leap of faith for me and is without a doubt the scariest thing I have ever done in my life. It's something I have agonized over for years and to have your support would mean the absolute world to me.

I do however understand that this could backfire completely. I understand that, as much as it breaks my heart, you may want to distance yourself from me for a while if you're having trouble dealing with it. Please know that this is the last thing I would want and I would love nothing better than to talk about it with you.

I like to think that this won't change a single thing. Most of my friends know, and I have received nothing but kindness from each and every one of them. There's also a whole load of other support out there – books, websites, leaflets etc. If you're interested – and nothing would make me happier than if you were – I can show you some really, really great places to look, as it might help if you feel like you want to understand things a little more. This is probably a huge shock so I want you to know that there's so much out there in terms of support and information for parents etc. Of course, you can also ask me – and I will be as honest with you as I can.

I want you two to know that I am at ease and secure with who I am. I also feel it necessary to cite something: this is not a choice. I have not chosen this, just like I did not choose to be blonde, to like the colour green, to have blue eyes, etc.

Please know that it would never be my intention to hurt you, and that I want nothing more than to make you happy and proud. You've both always been there for me and this is another reason why I have found it so difficult to tell you until now. I am so sorry if this causes you any pain or worry. You often tell me how proud you are of me and I hope that after this, you still feel the same way. I'm the same person I have always been, and nothing at all has changed about me or the way I am. I'm still your Lucy.

This is, undoubtedly, going to be a shock – so don't feel like you have to take it all in at once. I completely understand. I would love for you to reply, but only do so when you feel you are able to."

I swallowed. I knew they'd be sleeping – it was 11 p.m. – so now, all I could do was wait.

"I did it," I whispered.

"I am so, SO proud of you," Kaelyn said, grinning. "I wish I could give you the biggest hug ever right now. But you need to get some sleep! I'm sure they'll have replied by the time you wake up."

I nodded absent-mindedly, reading back through the email one last time, trying to figure out if I'd truly said everything I'd needed to say. I scrolled down to the very bottom of the page, and then something caught my eye. Underneath where I thought I'd ended the email, another sentence had appeared:

"I'll always love you, Mom and Dad. Love from, your son Ed."

I bit back a scream. I'd accidentally included a part of someone else's coming out email! I had forgotten to scroll down the whole way and remove the bits I hadn't used when I was copying and pasting from Google.

I started hyperventilating.

"Oh my GOD," I screeched. "OH. MY. GOD. WHAT HAVE I DONE? THEY'RE GOING TO

THINK I'M CALLED ED NOW. THEY'LL BE SO CONFUSED. THIS HAS RUINED EVERYTHING."

"It's OK, it's OK, it's OK," Kaelyn said. "They probably won't even notice. It's OK! Take a deep breath."

I started sobbing. I was so embarrassed. My parents were going to think I was mad!

My parents' response was the best that I could have possibly hoped for. They replied in the sweetest way, saying that they loved me no matter what, and that everything was going to be OK.

They already knew, of course. They'd guessed when letters from America had started arriving on the doorstep. I'd told them Kaelyn was just a friend, and they'd seen right through it but decided not to question me. That was what I loved about my parents – they were tactful and sensitive, and they'd put my happiness and comfort first. They knew I was going to tell them when I was ready. They still loved me. Nothing had changed. I had done it.

39 I'M NOT HOMOPHOBIC, BUT...

"Hey, guess what! I came out to my parents the other day," I said excitedly to Rex as we walked home from class one evening.

"Oh cool, congratulations."

"Thanks! I'm so relieved. It's such a weight off my shoulders, you know?"

"Yeah. I mean, I guess so."

We walked along in silence for a short while. "Can I ask you a question?" Rex said, tentatively.

"Sure?"

"Why do gay people feel the need to come out? Like, this is the twenty-first century. No one cares any more."

I was stunned. Did he hear what had just come out of his mouth? Did he know that what he'd said was offensive? I did my best to explain, trying to stay calm.

"Well, across the world, we're still being discriminated against. There are countries that don't even recognize our existence. We live in a world where we're assumed straight until told otherwise."

"No, you're not. Sure, you're the exception, because you don't *look* gay. But most LGBT people *do*. So why do you feel the need to tell everyone? Take gay men for example." He shuddered. "They're so flamboyant and in your face. I get it, they're gay and proud or whatever. But it's all they go on about. Gay this, gay that. Like I said, no one cares."

I felt like I'd been punched in the face. Every word that fell from his mouth was like a dagger in my chest, stabbing over and over again.

"No, you're wrong. People do care. People care enough to picket funerals. People care enough to stop us from getting married in some countries. People care enough to stop us having the same rights as everyone else, just because of who we love. So yes, coming out still matters. And it'll matter until we're able to live freely without persecution."

He stared at me. I could feel myself getting angrier and angrier. Now he'd got me going, I couldn't hold back.

"Do you even realize how much more 'straight' this world is than anything else?" I continued, feeling my face getting hot. "Every single movie I see, TV show I watch, and book I read, there is a man and a woman who fall in love. That's it."

"Probably because gay people flaunt that they're gay," he said. "No one wants to see that, because it's annoying to look at. Gays make a point of holding hands in the street and kissing each other all the time. It's unnecessary. I'm not homophobic, it's just irritating. End of."

"Gay people holding hands in the street isn't *flaunting*," I shouted. "They're just *existing*. I see thousands of straight couples holding hands in the street every single day. Is that them flaunting THEIR sexuality?"

He started walking away.

"You're an idiot," I yelled after him. "We come out because we're proud. We're ALLOWED to be proud. If we're not proud of ourselves, no one else would be."

I stomped home, seething. How dare he? I was so angry, I could barely speak. I had been so cocooned in a world of love and positivity that his reaction had shocked me to the core.

Us LGBT folk *are* courageous. By coming out, we are saying that we're ready to face any negative consequences that come our way. It's an act of defiance, and an act of pride, and it's something that should be applauded, not silenced.

I wish I had shouted this as Rex was walking away.

ANXIETY

Despite the way he had treated me, I continued to hang out with Rex because I didn't really have anyone else. And although he'd made a point of saying that he was fine with me being gay, he would frequently make comments that made me believe otherwise.

Kaelyn and I had been planning her trip to Plymouth for quite some time. She had two weeks off for Easter, and was going to come and visit me. I was so excited, and I'd been babbling about it to Rex when he suddenly interrupted me.

"Do you think you could stop talking about her so much? She's literally all you talk about. It's really annoying."

And so, I stopped. After all, Rex was the only friend I had in Plymouth. If I lost him, I would have nobody.

But I was starting to notice how quickly this toxic friendship was wearing me down. I was feeling increasingly miserable and cripplingly lonely, crying myself to sleep most nights, wishing I could be at home with my family and friends. I longed for Kaelyn to be there with me, to spur me on, but I knew that wasn't her job. I knew I couldn't rely on anyone else for happiness. I knew it had to come from within.

My anxiety was getting worse and worse. I felt sick to my stomach at the thought of leaving the house. I had started laying in bed all day, trying to stay calm, bribing my housemates to do my shopping for me. Just thinking about simple tasks, like going to the post office or walking to class, made me feel ill. All I wanted to do was curl up in my duvet and never come out.

I eventually convinced myself I needed to see a doctor. It took me three attempts to pick up the phone and make an appointment, but I managed it with shaking hands. The doctor was extremely understanding, and recommended that I take a six week course of Cognitive Behavioural Therapy. I was sceptical – was therapy the right choice for me? It all sounded a bit new age and hippy dippy. I went along to the first session with gritted teeth, expecting the worst. But as the session leader started talking about the symptoms of anxiety, I found myself nodding my head. I looked around the room. Everyone else was nodding, too. I began to relax. Maybe this was the right place for me, after all.

Gradually, we learned about how thought processes really work, and how, when we're feeling anxious, everything in our brain goes into overdrive. We had to learn to "catch" our anxious thoughts before they accumulated into something unmanageable. Half the time, the session leader said, anxiety about a situation comes from absolutely nothing.

"Catch the anxious thought, and ask yourself – is

this a realistic worry? What is the worst than can happen? And what if the worst *does* happen? Is it the end of the world? Usually, the answer is no."

Over the following weeks, I found myself growing steadily calmer again. My thoughts were clearing and my mind was quiet. When anxiety tried to rear its ugly head, I did my best to face it head on. *Is this a realistic thing to be panicking about?* I'd ask myself. The answer would always be no. All I had to do was step away from a situation, and remove the emotions attached to it. It was mind over matter, and slowly but surely, I was managing to get things back under control.

Meanwhile, I desperately wanted to make new friends so I could quietly drift away from Rex, but everyone in my class seemed to have already formed groups, and I felt like it was too late. So I struggled on, in the way I always have, absolutely certain that things would start getting better once Rex saw how badly he was treating me. I didn't realize that being friends with someone like him could only stretch you so far until you snap.

One evening, after a very stressful day of editing, I came home feeling exhausted and defeated. Rex had been angry at me over something all day, and it was wearing me thin. I was sick of having to tiptoe around him. I reached for my phone and texted Kaelyn, but she was about to go into surgery to operate on a dog, and there wasn't time to talk for long. I told her I loved her, that I was proud of her, and that I felt so lucky to have her by my side. I wished she could be there with me instead of thousands of miles away. I felt selfish, but I missed her, and I was so lonely.

I suddenly remembered something Ben had said to me all those years ago.

"Whenever either of us are feeling lonely, we should just look for the Big Dipper. It can be our little thing! A way to stop us feeling as lonely, even if we're far apart."

I went and stood by my window, and looked out at the night sky. I searched for the Big Dipper for ages, squinting through the glass, but I couldn't find it. All I could see was the glowing orange hue of the city skyline, lit up by the hundreds of street lamps. Feeling lonelier than ever, I turned away from the window, grabbed my phone and texted Emily and Bel.

Guys. I miss you all so much. Uni sucks big time right now. Save me!

Emily replied almost instantly.

Tell me about it. Some of my housemates are absolutely vile. Get me out of here please.

Bel chimed in.

Good to know I'm not the only one. Wish I could see you guys.

A feeling of nostalgia and sadness hit me like a ton of bricks. I missed my friends so much. I missed those carefree summers that we'd spent together, all the fun we'd had at the Village Players, and how comfortable and relaxed I felt when I was with them.

I started thinking about how different they were to Rex. Did I deserve to be treated this badly? No.

So why was I still being nice to him? Why were we still friends?

Because you're scared, said the little voice in my head, and I realized it was right. I've always hated conflict, and I tend to brush over things for the sake of staying positive and moving on. But I was starting to notice the huge difference between being nice and being passive. Sure, I could be kind, good-hearted and sympathetic, but I was certainly not passive. If it came to it, I could stand up for myself. Deep down, I knew I just needed to find the strength to walk away.

APRIL
2012

Kaelyn arrived in Plymouth at the end of April. I took her on the Ferris wheel, made her sample pasties for the first time ("meh, not as good as hamburgers") and showed her all the little beaches and restaurants. She loved the quaint Englishness of the city, and we decided that one day, maybe when we'd both finished studying, we would move to Devon or Cornwall together.

"It's just so peaceful," she said one evening as we sat together on the grass, looking out at the sea. I smiled. I couldn't wait to start my life with her.

One morning, I received a text message out of the blue from Rex, inviting Kaelyn and me to a barbecue at his house. I was over the moon – perhaps he had finally got over whatever it was that was bothering him? I could tell that Kaelyn wasn't so sure, but we went along anyway, armed with some sausages as a peace offering.

When we got there, the atmosphere was tense. Rex was busy trying to rekindle the burnt out barbecue, so we went inside and helped cook the food in the oven instead. He'd invited several other people from our film course, including the two girls I'd spotted on my first day. I saw my chance and went over to introduce myself.

The shorter girl, Leah, was really funny. She and Kaelyn got along brilliantly, and within minutes we were laughing and joking about whether or not we were all going to get food poisoning from our terrible cooking.

Kaelyn and I ambled home that evening hand in hand, our stomachs aching from how much Leah had made us laugh.

"You know, with people like Leah around, you don't really need to have someone like Rex in your life," said Kaelyn, tentatively. "Leah seems a lot more level-headed."

I knew Kaelyn was right. Suddenly I could see how truly harmful my friendship with Rex was, and how weird and twisted it had become. Rex had made me dislike parts of myself that I hadn't worried about since I was seventeen. It was time I cut the ties. Friends should lift you up, not pull you down.

And so, Rex and I drifted apart. It was difficult to walk away from the only real friend I'd made at university so far, but I knew it was for the best. I tried to stay positive, but it was tough. I felt lonely and scared, made worse by the fact that Kaelyn had to leave at the end of April to go back to America. Dropping her off at the airport was even more heartbreaking than before. I'd hoped saying goodbye would get easier as time went on. It didn't.

The only thing keeping me going was my

editing work. Kaelyn and I had decided to turn making montage videos of each of our trips into a little tradition. Being able to look back on all the adventures we'd had kept us going until the next time we saw each other. These little "films" helped to remind us that when we were together, nothing could stop us.

Once I'd finished editing our "April 2012" adventures, I uploaded it to YouTube, thinking nothing of it. We watched it together over Skype, trying to hold back our tears as we reminisced about what a wonderful trip it had been. We were so proud of how far we'd come.

When I woke up the next morning, I decided to log on to YouTube and watch the video one more time. But as the page loaded, I saw something that made my heart stop. The stat counter at the bottom of the page had sky-rocketed. The video had been viewed over 10,000 times! I scrolled down, open mouthed, and saw that we'd been left hundreds of new comments:

"You guys are seriously the cutest couple I have ever

seen, and I hope that one day I can be as happy with someone as you two are. Thank you for your videos."

I couldn't believe my eyes.

"You guys give me so much hope," another comment read. "Seeing the extraordinary love you two share, and the distance you've overcome? It makes me believe that my girlfriend and I can overcome homophobic parents and the horrors of high school. So thank you, thank you so much."

A few people had watched our videos before, but never this many. I was speechless. I couldn't believe that a twenty-minute montage video of two girls going out to eat at restaurants and making coffee together in the kitchen was helping people feel OK about themselves. Everyone was being so supportive, willing us on until our next trip together, telling us that we could make it and that they would be behind us all the way.

"I just feel so happy, proud and touched by this video. I wanted to thank you for proving to us that we are not alone! Keep on living this dream. You'll see each other again soon."

Kaelyn was just as surprised as I was. We were bewildered, but very flattered. It felt amazing to know that we had been able to help so many people just by being our weird, goofy selves.

"I feel like we should keep posting videos to this channel," Kaelyn said. "If we can make a tiny difference to all these people, then I don't see why not."

I agreed. "We could turn it into a little platform for LGBT people. Like a community kind of thing!"

A few weeks later, we decided to film our Coming Out stories. They were incredibly personal to us, yet people seemed to relate to them. Everyone was sharing their own stories in the comments section, giving advice to one another and offering up words of wisdom and support. It was incredible to read about what people were going through and what they had overcome.

This was our chance to make a difference.

It was my last night in Plymouth before the summer holidays began. I had the house to myself – everyone else had already left. As I cooked my dinner, I put on some John Mayer, turning the volume up to maximum, singing at the top of my lungs, dancing around the kitchen, miming into a spatula.

Sometimes things don't always go to plan, but that doesn't mean that life is terrible. My first year at university had been one of the toughest years of my life – but my struggles had allowed me to revamp everything I thought I knew about myself, and change for the better. Even if things weren't going my way, I had enough love and support from my friends and family to keep me going. I was independent, brave, and more confident and happy with myself than I had ever been.

My dad would be arriving the next day to take me home for the summer. As I was packing up all my things into boxes later that evening, folding sheets and pillowcases and taking down my posters, I kept turning that one J.K. Rowling quote over and over in my mind.

I'd been at rock bottom, but had slowly realized

that my only way out was to use the rocks around me to rebuild the steps and get back up again.

THE WORLD IS WATCHING

42

I hadn't been back to America since my trip with Becci and Clare, but now the summer holidays were here, I was finally on my way to visit Kaelyn in Michigan, her home town. I was nervous: I was going to meet her family for the first time!

I needn't have worried – they made me feel at ease instantly. We explored the local town together, walked Kaelyn's dogs in the park, and drank cocktails in the sunshine on her balcony. It struck me once again how different America was to anything I'd known before. Michigan was beautiful, much greener than I remember California being, and Kaelyn and I talked about living there one day before eventually moving to England for good and raising a family. It was exciting to talk about the future together.

Whenever I was with Kaelyn, it was as if all my worries and anxieties were put on hold. We were in a little bubble where nobody could touch us, and saying goodbye was like crashing back down to earth. Each time we left each other, the bubble would burst, and it ripped my heart to shreds.

When I uploaded *"August 2012"* to YouTube later on that week, we received a flurry of support. The video hit 100,000 views in just a few days, and we were completely blown away by the sudden surge in interest. The emotional endings to our videos, where we said goodbye to each other at the airport, seemed to strike a particular chord with people. They loved being able to count down with us until our next trip, spurring us on with messages of love and support.

We felt a sense of pressure, now that we had a fairly large viewership, to act a certain way. People started writing to us, telling us that we were their role models – something we just could not wrap our heads around – and it was terrifying to know that there were people out there who looked up to us even though we'd never met them. One particular letter we received was from a nine-year-old girl in Kansas, which simply read: *"If you two break up, I'll never believe in love again."* I was horrified. I didn't want anyone to base their idea of what love should be on my relationship alone. Suddenly, we had a huge weight of responsibility on our shoulders.

Neither Kaelyn nor I could figure out what made us so special. We were just two girls having fun, sharing little snippets of our lives online. And although the idea of being a role model was a strange one, as we didn't feel like we'd done anything particularly outstanding, we knew that all we could do was to try and be the best possible versions of ourselves, and stay true to what we believed in.

People were sending us letters from all over the world, and we made a point of writing back to everyone, no matter how long it took. It felt wonderful to read such kind-hearted messages of support, but every now and then, we'd receive a letter that would send shivers down my spine. A twenty-three-year-old girl living in Russia had snuck into her local library in the dead of night to write to us, terrified that her parents would find the letter if she wrote it at home. She told us that when she'd plucked up the courage to come out to her best friend, her friend had told her that she was disgusting and was going to hell. *"People like me can get killed here for being who we are,"* she wrote. *"Sometimes I'm scared for my life."*

One morning, a brown paper package wrapped up tightly with string arrived all the way from Saudi Arabia. The girl who'd written it had asked someone to smuggle the letter out of the country for her, for fear that customs would open it, read that she was gay, and have her killed. She told us that she'd attempted suicide twice, and that our videos were the only thing that kept her going. *"Your videos keep me strong when I don't think I can make it any more. I watch them in the dead of night. Thank you for giving me hope that things will get better for me."* I stared at the page with shaking hands, stunned, trying not to cry. I was entirely lost for words.

It was chilling. The things I was reading in those letters went so far beyond my own extremely sheltered experiences. I was astonished by the sheer strength, bravery and courage that people showed, despite their devastating circumstances. It was truly humbling to read their words. Their stories opened my eyes to the world, and showed me what was beyond the walls of my own privileged existence.

And then, one afternoon, by some strange yet wonderful twist of fate, Chely Wright stumbled across my Coming Out story on YouTube. The same Chely Wright who had been on the Ellen Show. The same Chely Wright whom seventeen-year-old me had been inspired by that warm summer evening all those years ago.

She tweeted me:

"Hi Lucy. I want you to know how deeply touched I was as I watched your video this morning. Knowing that you were out there, and that you heard me on Ellen's

show, well – it made me cry tears of joy. And now, seeing you passing the torch to others is just exactly the way it should work. You are a beacon of hope and light for so many. Your fan, Chely xo."

I burst into tears. I was speechless. How she had found it, I didn't know – but it seemed like everything had come full circle, and I was completely overwhelmed. This woman had helped me accept myself for who I was . . . and now *she* was congratulating *me*, for what *I* had achieved.

I felt so happy as I went to bed that night. Sometimes, life has a funny way of making sure things fall into place.

By September, after a summer of hanging out with my family and my old friends, I was beginning to really look forward to going back to Plymouth. I'd been talking to Leah all summer, and I was so excited to see her again. I'd also moved into a new house; number 115 Mount Gould Road. Grace had moved in with me, along with a guy named Phil, from Northern Ireland – who turned out to be one of the funniest people I'd ever met. Within twenty minutes, we were laughing like we'd known each other for years. Phil and Leah quickly became my closest friends at university. On evenings when we weren't working, we would hang out at one of our favourite haunts, the Caffeine Club, which sold monster milkshakes topped with whipped cream and chocolate pieces, and giant burgers the size of our faces.

I threw myself head first into my second year at university. I started working on commissions and taking on extra projects, and I began to feel really proud of the work I was producing. I made several short documentaries, wrote two full screenplays, and managed another year of "firsts". I had found my niche, and I loved the creativity that came with making a film from start to finish. I couldn't believe how much easier things were when I was doing something I cared about, surrounded by people who were right for me.

I was finally comfortable and happy with where I was headed.

I CAN MAKE YOU STRAIGHT

43

Of course, no matter where you're headed in life, you're always going to come across people who are determined to bring you down.

One afternoon, during our lunch break, a guy from my course named Karl sauntered up to me with a smirk.

"Yo. I saw your video."

"What video?" I said, intrigued.

"Your Coming Out video on YouTube. One million views, huh?"

"Oh! Yeah. I can't believe that many people have seen it!"

"So you're gay then?" he said, his eyes

narrowing, holding my gaze.

I shifted on my feet nervously. "Yeah, I am." I looked him dead in the eye, preparing for the worst.

There was a long pause. "What a waste, man." He stared at me, unblinking, waiting for a reaction.

I raised one eyebrow. I wasn't going to get angry. Rex had prepared me for this: I had my comebacks down to a tee. "That's kind of rude, don't you think?" I said, calmly. "I mean, how do you think that makes me feel? To be told I'm waste?"

"I'm not trying to offend you, man. I'm just saying. You chose the wrong path."

"I didn't choose this, any more than you chose to be straight, Karl."

"Whatever, dude. It's just such a waste. Give me time and I can make you straight."

I couldn't hold back my laughter. I couldn't believe how ignorant and insecure he sounded. It takes a certain type of person to try and provoke others for their own sordid enjoyment. I turned and left the room, smiling.

Over the summer, I attended Chicago Pride with Kaelyn. We spent the day marching through Chicago surrounded by thousands of other like-minded people, cheering and whooping. As we walked the city streets hand in hand, I suddenly noticed how 'normal' it felt. Having spent years feeling like I stuck out like a sore thumb, it was incredible to feel like I now *fit*. The fact that I was different was no longer a big deal.

People like Karl were old news. I was so happy and comfortable with myself that nothing anyone could say about my sexuality was going to get to me any more. It had taken me a long time to be OK with labelling myself as gay and being out and proud about it, and now, nothing could change that.

44 RESPECT

We had been planning something huge for our YouTube viewers for a while now. We'd just hit 15 million views, and to celebrate, we decided to hold a meet-up, where people could come and hang out with others in the LGBT community in a safe environment, get to know each other, and dissolve the feeling of isolation that so many people experience when they're coming to terms with who they are.

We held the event in London, and six hundred people turned up. I hugged each and every one of them, took photos with every single one of them, and shared stories and advice. It was the most wonderful, heart-warming experience. Later on in the day, a girl came up to us, crying, thanking us for giving her a space where she could feel comfortable, happy and be honest about her sexuality for the first time, without having to worry about receiving backlash or nasty comments.

"You and Kaelyn are my ultimate role models," she smiled, wiping away her tears. "You make me feel so much better, just by existing. I know that sounds silly, but it's true. The world needs more people like you two – just normal people living their lives, who just happen to be gay. Thank you."

I wanted to cry. I was so flattered and overwhelmed. I'd never imagined that the struggles I'd had with my own sexuality would lead to something like this. I thought about what seventeen-year-old Lucy would have said, if she could see me now. I knew she would be so proud.

A few weeks later, *Diva* magazine asked Kaelyn and me if we wanted to be on their next cover, alongside two of our best friends, Whitney and Megan, who also made YouTube videos. Whitney was from America and Megan was from England, and we had so much in common with them. They'd been a long-distance couple, too, before finally closing the gap and moving in together in 2012, before having their civil partnership later on that year.

The cover shoot was so surreal. We had our hair and make-up done by professionals, and spent all afternoon shooting, trying on dozens of different outfits. It felt very empowering to be in a room full of such successful, hard-working women who were so talented at their jobs. We were still getting used to the idea of being asked to give interviews for magazines – and being on the *cover* of one felt even stranger.

We were amazed at how many opportunities simply being on YouTube had presented to us. Companies were now asking us to help promote their products, and started sending us all kinds of weird and wonderful things: pink hair extensions made from sheep's wool, stuffed dolls made to look exactly like us, and a strange selection of miniature garden gnomes. . .

What amazed us even more was how many wonderful people we were meeting. We had met Whitney and Megan online, but we quickly became fantastic friends beyond the realms of YouTube. We had so much in common, and they were always there for us. They'd been through a long-distance relationship and had come out the other side stronger than ever, so they knew exactly what it felt like.

"Distance is always worth it when you're in love," I remember Whitney saying to us once. "I mean, you'd have to be mad to assume that your soulmate lives ten minutes down the road from you!"

When Kaelyn and I were finding the separation tough, they'd always be there to cheer us on, sending us little letters and packages to help keep us going. "You can do it, girls," they'd say. "Just a few more months until you see each other again!"

As time passed, we started getting to know some other members of the YouTube community.

We became really close with Katy and Eilis, a long-distance couple from Scotland. They were some of the funniest, smartest people we had ever met, and pretty soon we were texting back and forth every day, swapping hilarious stories and sharing advice with one another. We also got to know Jelly and Day, a couple from Texas, who had the most wonderful sense of humour and were so genuine and supportive. A whole new world had been opened up to us, and it was amazing to listen and learn about what these people had been through and how they had overcome their struggles. It was even more amazing to watch them do their bit for the LGBT community, giving out advice and offering up support. Hearing their stories had opened my eyes to how far we still have to go until we reach true equality, and I vowed right then and there to be the best possible role model I could be.

My last year of university was coming to an end. Leah and I had just finished our final major project, and we had come to Maritimo's, our favourite tapas bar, to celebrate.

We sat outside on the restaurant patio by the seafront. The sun was setting, and the sky was a deep, fiery pink. It was peaceful, but it was also sad. I couldn't believe how fast the year had gone.

The waiter arrived with our cocktails. He presented them to us flamboyantly, flicking the tea towel over his shoulder for effect. We laughed.

"He's the kind of guy Karl would have a real problem with," I whispered with a grin as he turned away.

Leah smiled. "Karl is messed up. He's so backwards. Virtually no one here has opinions like his any more. He's from the dark ages, I swear."

We sat in silence for a while, sipping on our cocktails. Then Leah spoke up. "I really respect gay people, you know?"

"I really respect gay people, too," I said, smirking.

She burst out laughing. "No, but seriously. I can't imagine what you've gone through. For me, it was so easy. I fancied boys, and that was that.

It must have been so much scarier for you, not to have those feelings. I know it must have been so confusing and lonely." She paused, frowning. "I respect that, I really do."

Her words, however throwaway or casual they had been for her, made me so happy. To know that I could be openly gay and still respected by my friends and family made me feel all warm and fuzzy. Sometimes a little reassurance can go a really long way.

University had been three years of wonderful highs and devastating lows, but the ups and downs had made me a stronger, better, more well-rounded person. I had a degree under my belt. I'd come to appreciate the true value of friendship. I had a better grasp of what it meant to be a feminist. I realized that the people who don't value you don't matter. I learned about the importance of doing what's right, of having a say, and of standing up for yourself. Most importantly, after years of having absolutely no self-esteem, I had finally learned to love myself. That has been my biggest achievement to date.

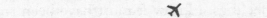

It was my last night in Plymouth, and once again, I was the only one left in the house. As dusk fell, I opened my bedroom window as wide as it could go, and breathed in the city air. A bar fight had broken out just down the road, and beyond the hysterical screeches I could hear the soft rumble of car engines and the distant coo of seagulls. I realized how much I was going to miss Plymouth, in all its grey, rainy glory. I looked up and spotted the Big Dipper, shining bright above the rooftops, majestic and aloof. I grabbed my phone and texted Ben.

He replied almost instantly. *I can see it, too. We're never too far apart, are we?!*

I put my phone away and sighed. I felt so happy.

"You did it," I said out loud. "You've made it this far."

NO MORE COUNTDOWNS

Kaelyn and I had been making plans to move in together for a while. All we had to figure out was when, where and how. Now that I'd finished university, the "when" had been taken care of – we wanted to do it as soon as possible.

Kaelyn had finished her veterinary training and had been looking for an internship. She finally landed a spot at an emergency animal clinic in Phoenix, Arizona. The clinic had a great reputation, and I was so proud of her for getting a place. And so, just like that, we decided that I would move to Arizona to be with her.

From the outside, making the choice to move

to the other side of the world seemed easy. We had been long distance for four whole years, and all we wanted was to be together, with no more countdowns, tears or goodbyes. I knew that moving to a new continent would be life-changing in the best possible way – but that didn't stop it from being petrifying.

I knew that I was going to miss home terribly. I also was going to miss the "English-ness" of life in the UK. All of the home comforts that I took for granted – cups of tea, Yorkshire puddings, Marmite – would be gone. What was life going to be like in Phoenix? How would I adjust to driving on the other side of the road? Was I going to melt in the Arizona climate?

Kaelyn and I had always known that one of us would eventually have to leave her home country. We also knew that we'd probably both have to do it over the course of our lives, depending on where we ended up. So although I was nervous, my desire for adventure was stirring. I've always believed that, every so often, a huge change is a positive thing. It keeps you sharp and alert, and stops you from resting on your laurels. I'd lived in Plymouth for three years, and I knew it was time to move on to pastures new.

But nothing had prepared me for how hard it was to say goodbye to my family and friends. I had just two months before my move to Arizona in the summer, and I was determined to make the most of every second. I spent my days cycling around my village and having picnics in the sunshine with my friends, padding barefoot through golden corn fields and swimming in the River Windrush. In the evenings, I sat in my garden with my family, listening to the bees and watching the honeysuckle billow in the wind.

During my last week in England, Becci and Clare presented me with a photo album. They'd selected all of our best moments – school break times, parties, shopping trips and restaurant outings, and finally, clips from our adventures in America. Each snap had its own special caption. It was such a beautiful gesture.

One evening in early August, I met with a few friends from school to see a film at the Phoenix Picturehouse, a tiny art house cinema in the middle of Oxford. Before we went inside, we headed out into Jericho for some late-night snacks from G&D's, our favourite ice cream cafe. As we sat outside at the little metal tables, I looked down at my mint-chocolate-chip ice cream cone, with its two flakes and its sticky toffee sauce, and realized just how much I was going to miss Oxford. Not just the people – or the ice cream – but the place itself. The university buildings jutted high out into the sky, their elegant structures a dark silhouette against the sunset and the street lamps. Somewhere in the distance, bells were chiming. The air was unusually warm, and people were spilling out into the street from the restaurant opposite, laughing and joking, clinking their glasses. There was a reason that poet Matthew Arnold called it "the city of dreaming spires." My city was beautiful, and it was home. I was going to miss it so much.

On one of my last days in England, the local news announced that there was going to be a Perseids meteor shower. As my friends and I gathered together in the fields, huddled under blankets, trying to spot shooting stars, I silently made a wish whenever one whizzed by.

I hope my life is always as happy as this.

Finally, August 15th arrived. As the plane took off, I watched my tiny country shrink smaller and smaller into the distance until it was blocked by a wall of thick white cloud. I cleared my throat and stared straight ahead. My mind began to clear. I was terrified, but at the same time, I was strangely calm. I was off to start a new life, with someone I adored, and I was as ready as I was ever going to be.

ARE YOU TWO A COUPLE?

46

"I'll just have a water, please!"

"What?"

"A water."

"An . . . a what? Orange juice?"

"WA-TER! H_2O! The stuff that comes out of taps!"

Despite what people may believe, America and England are very, very different places. I immediately discovered that people really struggled to understand my accent. Ordering a simple "glass of water, please" was like pulling teeth. Everyone assumed I was Australian.

I also had to adjust to American-style TV.

"ARE YOU SUFFERING FROM BAD GAS?"

Adverts would scream at me from across the room.

"DO YOU STRUGGLE WITH UNTIMELY
BOWEL MOVEMENTS?"

And while road signs in Britain say gentle things like, "Don't drive drunk!" and "Please be safe and responsible when driving," Arizonian road signs are a little more direct:

"DRIVE HAMMERED, GET NAILED."

I felt lonely at first, and disorientated. I was a country girl at heart, and the bustling streets of the Phoenix metropolis were far flung from the narrow country lanes I was used to strolling along, avoiding rabbits and dodging pheasants. But despite the huge differences, it felt good to be somewhere new, and I loved being able to explore another part of the world. It was an adventure.

Family life with Kaelyn was one thing I got used

to very quickly. As always when you move in with someone for the first time, we started learning a lot more about each other. She was the kind of girl who ate sandwiches over the sink for every meal just to save washing up, but I managed to convince her that a diet of peanut butter, jam and white bread probably wasn't doing her any good. We started cooking together, testing out weird and wonderful recipes (which would often end in disaster), flicking tomato sauce at each other while the cats played at our feet. I learned that she had a penchant for ice cream sandwiches (she ended up making a dedicated storage space in our freezer), and that she snored herself awake most nights (just kidding, Kae! Kind of. . .).

One thing I had been really wary of since moving out there was the way LGBT people were treated in a conservative place like Arizona, but neither Kaelyn nor I noticed anything significant. We could still walk down the street holding hands without any trouble, and the worst we would get were a few glares every now and then.

One week in early November, Kaelyn and I took a trip up to Flagstaff, a sleepy little city in northern Arizona. When we went to check in at the hotel reception, the lady behind the desk kept looking up at us and grinning as she typed in our details. She handed us our room key without a word, but suddenly spoke up as we turned to leave.

"Hang on a minute!"

Kaelyn and I looked at each other nervously. Checking into hotel rooms as a couple was often uncomfortable, because people had a habit of being intrusive. We braced ourselves for the worst.

"Are you two . . . *a couple*?"

"Yes."

The woman started banging her fists on the table, squealing excitedly. We jumped back in surprise.

"I knew it! I knew it!" She hurried around the desk and came rushing at us, pulling us into an embrace. When she drew back, we saw that she had tears in her eyes.

"My daughter ... she is just like you. She came out to me just a few months back. Oh, I love her so much. I'm so proud of her. And I'm so happy for you girls! God bless you both. Have a wonderful stay!"

Once I'd officially launched my website, offering up my services as a freelance film and video editor, I landed a job pretty quickly and really began coming into my own. I could feel myself settling down, finding a routine, and sticking to it. When I wasn't editing, I spent my time writing this book. It was therapeutic and strangely calming, setting my little life out into chapters and paragraphs, analysing every last detail, bullet pointing my memories in chronological order like they were ingredients in a recipe.

And this brings me up to now.

Today is April 19th. It's 7:34 p.m., almost dusk,

and I'm sitting here on my balcony with my feet up, sipping on a glass of wine, peering out at the glittering highway between the gap in the apartment buildings opposite ours. It's busy, and it's noisy, but something about it feels like home.

I love it here in Arizona. My ghostly English skin has slowly become used to the sunburn and the freckles. I've adjusted to the hot, dusty climate. We live in a gorgeous third floor apartment with a pool, a gym and dozens of elegant palm trees which tower above us, swaying in the wind. The views from our window are breathtaking. We live in the valley, surrounded by majestic, sandy mountains, their craggy peaks soaring up into the vibrant blue sky. It's new, it's different, and it's scary – but so was Plymouth, and that turned out just fine. Kaelyn and I finally have the life we so desperately wanted. We have three cats – Alfie, Oscar and Isaac – and we're a happy little family. (Isaac is my favourite though – don't tell the others!)

I feel like I've come an awfully long way. I was such a shy, anxious child, and as a teen all I wanted was to blend into the crowd. I denied myself the chance to be authentic for so long, but I'm now at a place in my life where I can comfortably be *me* – truly, utterly, completely *me*.

I'm also in a position to spread the message of equality on a much wider scale. We have hundreds of thousands of people following us on social media, where we do our best to preach love and acceptance over hated, bigotry and homophobia. Our videos on YouTube have been viewed over 25 million times. We've had interviews published in *The Guardian*, *The Hairpin*, *The Washington Blade*, *The Hush Project*, *Glamour* magazine, *Flurt* magazine, *Diva* magazine and *The Huffington Post*. We've held LGBT meet-ups in London, Detroit, Chicago and Phoenix. We've tried our best to utilize our internet platform as a community building tool, to bring together groups of people who can talk to one another when they need a friend, some advice, or simply a shoulder to cry on.

Kaelyn and I receive hundreds of letters a week from people who have gone through everything you could possibly imagine. Their stories are heartfelt, inspiring, upsetting and painful. We laugh with them, we cry with them, and we find ourselves in awe, time and time again, by the sheer strength, tenacity and courage that they show. The message of these stories is always clear: love wins over hate, every single time.

And then I realize that it's stories that have kept me alive. Fact or fiction, real-life or fantasy, they've made me who I am today. From the magical world of witches, wizards and colour catching, to Chely Wright's story of survival, acceptance and self-love, these narratives have encouraged me, motivated me, and kept me going.

Sharing stories is an inherently human thing. We pass them down from generation to generation, and something about the way they're told keeps us coming back for more. For every person on this planet, there's a story that's waiting to be heard, shared or retold. For each of those stories, there will be something that stands out – maybe a sentence or phrase, or even just a word – something that sticks with you. This is the phrase you mull over in difficult times. This is the sentence you think about to spur yourself on when the going gets tough. This is the word you get tattooed on your body, or printed on a poster, or worn around your wrist on a bracelet. Because this is the reason we tell stories. We tell them to survive.

It's surreal to think of how far I've come, and how on earth I've ended up here, in this exact spot. I like to think that it's because I have *inner strength*, and maybe that's partly it, but I know it's not the only reason. Life has thrown its fair share of craziness at me, and I've dealt with it as best I could – but I've been lucky. Very lucky. When I'm finding life hard and nothing seems to be going my way, I've always reached out to the people that are closest to me. And time and time again, I'm reminded of how much I am loved, how much I love, and how important love is, because it really does make the world go round.

Who are your top LGBTQA role models?
Ellen Page is someone I have looked up to for years! She's so intelligent and articulate.

What's the most important piece of advice you would give to someone who is planning to come out to friends and family?
Make sure you're doing it because you feel comfortable doing so, and not because someone else is pressuring you. Rehearse what you want to say beforehand, stay calm, and remember that as long as you love yourself, you don't need approval from anyone else.

What's your favourite thing about living in the US?
The fact that I can get Chipotle delivered to my door, any time of day or night.

What do you miss most about the UK?
My family, my friends and marmite.

Where would your and Kaelyn's dream date take place?
We both love calm, quiet places, so probably a nice secluded beach that has margaritas on tap.

What's the most annoying thing about Kaelyn?
She never throws anything away. There is a bag of clothes and shoes in our wardrobe that are from when she was NINE. Those shoes aren't gonna fit you anymore, Kaelyn, no matter how hard you squish those toes...

What annoys her about you?
I went in the other room to ask her this and she

just looked at me and whispered, "Everything." I think she was joking. I think.

Do you have any celeb crushes?
Ellen Page, Taylor Swift, Shay Mitchell, Gillian Anderson... the list is never-ending, to be honest!

What's your most embarrassing moment?
I repeatedly wear my clothes inside out and/or back to front, and not realize for the entire day. The number of times I've looked in the mirror and thought, Hang on a second...

What's your best quality?
I'm very loyal, and I'm really good at doing accents.

Do you have any nicknames for Kaelyn?
I call her Bubba Squibbs. One day I'm gonna put it on a T-shirt and make her wear it.

Who would you like to play you in the movie of your life?

I've lost count of how many times I've been told I look like Emily Kinney. So probably her – or maybe Dakota Fanning.

What's your guiltiest pleasure?
ABBA.

What is your greatest fear?
That I'll get appendicitis on a plane. I'm also terrified of velvet.

If you had to describe yourself in three words, what would they be?
Crazy cat lady.

What single thing would you take with you to a desert island?
One of those really obnoxiously shaped pool floats. I saw one in the supermarket the other day shaped like a pretzel. That's the only thing anyone would ever truly need on a desert island.

ACKNOWLEDGEMENTS

I'd like to thank my editors at Scholastic, Helen, Emily and Sam, for their expert help throughout the creation of this book. Your advice and support has propelled this project forwards in ways I could never have imagined, and I'm so grateful to the three of you for believing in me and this crazy idea!

Kaelyn – you've been my absolute rock for the last six years and I wouldn't have made it this far without you. Thank you for being the best thing that's ever been mine. Here's to taking on the world together.

I'd also like to thank each and every one of my friends. Thank you for being so utterly, unconditionally supportive right from the get go. I'm not sure what I did to deserve such wonderful people in my life, but I'm so incredibly grateful that you all exist. Here's to many more nights spent in our local pub, crowded around a single packet of Wotsits.

And lastly, I'd like to thank my cats. I know you can't read, but the three of you were always in the room when I was writing this book so I feel like, in a way, you wrote it with me. Sort of. Thanks for sitting on my laptop keys when I was trying to type, ripping up pages and pages of my notes with your teeth when I wasn't looking, and attacking my face and hair when I tried to pet your bellies. That's true love right there.